The Organic Building Up of the Church

as the Body of Christ to be the Organism of the Processed and Dispensing Triune God

Witness Lee

Living Stream Ministry
Anaheim, CA • www.lsm.org

First Edition, December 1989.

ISBN 978-0-87083-497-4

Published by

Living Stream Ministry
2431 W. La Palma Ave., Anaheim, CA 92801 U.S.A.
P. O. Box 2121, Anaheim, CA 92814 U.S.A.

Printed in the United States of America

10 11 12 13 14 / 11 10 9 8 7 6

CONTENTS

PREFACE

This small book is composed of messages given by Brother Witness Lee during the weekend of November 23-25, 1989, in Anaheim, California.

CHAPTER ONE

THE INTRINSIC ESSENCE OF THE CHURCH FOR ITS ORGANIC EXISTENCE

Scripture Reading: 1 John 1:2; 5:1; John 3:3, 5-6; 1:12-13; 3:29-30; Gen. 2:21-23; John 12:24; 1 Pet. 1:3; Rom. 8:29; Heb. 2:11-12; John 15:1, 5, 16, 8; Eph. 1:22-23; Rom. 12:5; 1 Cor. 10:32; 12:28; Eph. 3:19b; Rev. 1:4a, 11

OUTLINE

I. The intrinsic essence of the church:
  A. The divine life, which generates the church—1 John 1:2; 5:1:
    1. By the regeneration of the Spirit in the believers' spirit—John 3:3, 5-6.
    2. Making them the children of God as the bride of Christ, who is the Bridegroom, for His increase, as typified by Eve as the counterpart to Adam—John 1:12-13; 3:29-30; Gen. 2:21-23.
  B. Through the release of the divine life by Christ as the one grain of wheat falling into the ground and dying there for His multiplication—John 12:24.
  C. Through the impartation of the divine life by Christ as the firstborn Son of God in His resurrection, that God may have many sons as the many brothers of Christ—1 Pet. 1:3; Rom. 8:29; Heb. 2:11-12.
  D. The many brothers of Christ being His many branches grafted into Him, the true vine in the universe, to bear much fruit for His enlargement in His spreading, that they might express the Triune God as His organism—John 15:1, 5, 16, 8.

    E. This organism of the Triune God being the organic Body of Christ, constituted with His many brothers as the many members of His organic Body—Eph. 1:22-23; Rom. 12:5.

II. The organic existence of the church:

    A. Existing in the universe as the one universal church of God for His universal expression, the fullness of God—1 Cor. 10:32; 12:28; Eph. 3:19b.

    B. Spreading in many localities on the earth as many local churches to be His local expressions—Rev. 1:4a, 11.

THE INTRINSIC ESSENCE OF THE CHURCH
FOR ITS ORGANIC EXISTENCE

Prayer: Lord, how we thank You for this Thanksgiving weekend conference. May this conference be a real thanksgiving from us to You. Lord, cover us with Your precious blood. How much we need Your blood and Your anointing, the rich anointing with all the unsearchable riches of the Triune God. Lord, we thank You for the past. Thank You for the present. We even thank You for the coming days. Lord, be with us. We need Your presence. Lord, anoint the whole meeting. Anoint every attendant. Lord, open the heavens and give us a clear sky that we may have a clear view under Your oracle. Take away all the veils, take away all the clouds, and give us Your own revelation. We want to see something. We want not only to hear, but also to see. Lord Jesus, we love You, and we want to see You in this meeting. We want to be touched by You. Touch us, Lord. Touch each one of us, and give to each one of us the particular word that we need. Lord, we thank You again that You are so sovereign. You are on the throne. We worship You, and we give You all the glory, yet we still remember Your enemy. Lord, we are fighting against him. We are always in the battle. Lord, fight the battle for us. Put him aside, and shame him. May all the glory be to You. Lord, may all the blessings be bestowed upon us. Thank You for the church. Thank You for Your oracle today. Speak in our speaking. Lord, we believe You are one with us, one spirit with us, and we believe we are one spirit with You. Thank You for this oneness. We pray in Your mighty name. Amen.

My burden in these messages concerns five intrinsic things. Four concern the church, and one concerns the winds of teaching. The first four intrinsic things of the church are: the intrinsic essence of the church for its organic existence; the intrinsic growth of the church for its organic increase; the intrinsic building up of the church for its organic function; and the intrinsic fellowship of the churches for their organic relationship. The intrinsic essence, the intrinsic growth, the intrinsic building up, and the intrinsic fellowship are all very positive. The last intrinsic factor of the winds of teaching for their evil purpose is a negative item.

THE INTRINSIC ESSENCE OF THE CHURCH

When we speak of the essence of anything, we are referring to its most intrinsic part. Regarding the church, the most important positive factor is its intrinsic essence. Many in Christianity have made the church something outward. When some speak of the church, they mean a physical building. If they speak of going to church, they mean going to a chapel or cathedral or some kind of sanctuary. These are material things constructed of bricks, stones, steel, or wood. What a mistake this is! While others are somewhat improved in their concept, they still pay too much attention to the outward aspects of the church, such as its organization. Many Christians are experiencing conflicts with each other today because they are in the realm of the outward factors rather than centering on the intrinsic essence of the church. Instead of being one with one another to fight against God's enemy, many Christians are divided and even fighting one another. This is similar to the fighting among the nations of the world. The United Nations was formed with the intention to unite the nations, but throughout the years, there have only been division and fighting among them.

We need to see that the church is one. It is the only church of the unique God. This church is the unique Body of Christ, and Christ is the Head of this Body. In John 17 the Lord prayed that we all might be one (John 17:11, 21-23), but if we look at Christian history throughout the past nineteen centuries, we will find that the Christians have been fighting one another. The strange thing is that if we Christians had never come together, we would have no fighting. If there had been no marriage, there would be no divorce. Every divorce had its beginning with a dear, sweet, precious marriage.

I have been a Christian for sixty-four years. From the time that I began to meet with other Christians, I have witnessed much fighting. The closer we are to one another, the more of a tendency we have to fight with one another. Those who love each other can become enemies. Hatred can replace love, and jealousy can replace sympathy. This is today's situation in Christianity. What a shame this is! Why has so much fighting taken place on this earth among Christians for so many centuries? It is because the Christians have turned from the intrinsic essence of the church to something outward.

There are four intrinsic matters of the church. The first of these is the essence of the church. Then the growth of the church is also intrinsic. If a tree grows, it grows in its intrinsic part. Following the growth is the building up of the church. The fourth intrinsic element of the church is its fellowship. The essence, the growth, the building up, and the fellowship are all very intrinsic. If every Christian remained in these four intrinsic matters, we would have no problems. Whenever we turn from the intrinsic matters to something that we can touch outwardly and that we can see outwardly, we are on the way to "divorce." This is because all the outward, physical things are dividing factors.

If we learn this lesson and receive the grace of the Lord, we will say, "Lord, save me! Rescue me and turn me from the outward to the intrinsic." Then immediately we will be one. This is why I am so burdened to fellowship about these four crucial things: the intrinsic essence, the intrinsic growth, the intrinsic building up, and the intrinsic fellowship.

The Divine Life, Which Generates the Church

The divine life, God's life, the eternal life, the uncreated life, the indestructible life, is the very essence of the church, and this divine life generates the church (1 John 1:2; 5:1). Of course, we cannot see this divine life, just as we are not able to see the steel in this meeting hall. This is because the steel is covered by stones and wood, yet the steel is the very essence of this building's structure.

The essence of the church is the divine life, and the divine life is Christ as the very embodiment of the processed Triune God (John 14:6; Col. 2:9). God was just God in eternity past, but one day the entire God, the complete God in the second person of His divine Trinity, became incarnated. Incarnation is a wonderful process whereby God entered into man. The Triune God entered into a human virgin's womb and stayed there for nine months. It was by this wonderful process that He put man upon Himself and that He Himself became a man. God with His divine Trinity was embodied in a man. That man, by the name of Jesus of Nazareth, was a real, perfect, and genuine man, yet His very intrinsic essence was God. He is both God and man, the God-man. This wonderful man lived on this earth for thirty-three and a half years. He lived in a carpenter's home, and He Himself was a carpenter (Matt. 13:55; Mark 6:3). How wonderful it is that the Triune God in this man sawed wood and did carpentry work! This was His human living for thirty years.

When He was thirty years of age, He came out to minister. In His ministry, He had to deal with "troublesome" ones like Peter and the sons of thunder, James and John (Mark 3:17). I do not know why the Lord Jesus did not choose disciples who were all wise, rich, and educated. Instead, some of those He chose were fishermen from Galilee. They were peculiar and rough like Peter. The Lord even chose Judas Iscariot, who became His betrayer. After the Lord's betrayal, He was arrested, but actually, He voluntarily entered into death (John 10:17-18). He bore the cross, and He went to the cross to die an all-inclusive death to solve all of our problems and all of God's problems. He resurrected and then ascended to another realm, the third heaven, where He still is today (Eph. 4:10; Heb. 4:14; 1:3; cf. 2 Cor. 12:2).

God passed through all these processes to become someone who can carry out the dispensing. This is why we say that the church is the organism of the processed and dispensing Triune God. The very God whom we worship is a processed God. He has been processed in order to be a dispensing One. Our God is now the processed Triune God to be a dispensing God. Today He does not need to pass through any other process. What He is doing today is dispensing Himself into man. We should not forget that without God being processed, there is no ground for Him to dispense Himself into us. His passing through the processes was for Him to be a dispensing God.

Because He is the dispensing God, He is able to regenerate us, and this regenerating life is the divine life. The term "divine life" is simple, but the implication of this term is not that simple. The divine life is the dispensing God, who is the very essence of the church. We all can testify that when we were first saved, we were always happy to meet another saved one. Many times we became more intimate with one another than with our fleshly brothers and sisters. We Christians love one another because we have the same essence. It does not matter whether we are American, European, Chinese, Japanese, Korean, white, black, yellow, brown, or red. As long as we are real Christians, we have a loving essence within us. When we turn away from this intrinsic essence to touch other things, we begin to fight one another. After we have been together for a while, problems may begin to arise over outward things. In order to solve the problems between Christians, we must come to the intrinsic matters of the church: first, the intrinsic essence; second, the intrinsic growth; third, the intrinsic building up; and fourth, the intrinsic fellowship. We are safeguarded in these four intrinsic matters.

The intrinsic essence of the church is the divine life that the processed Triune God has dispensed and is now dispensing into us. The divine life generates us by the regeneration of the Spirit in our spirit. The divine Spirit begets the human spirit (John 3:3, 5-6). How wonderful it is that these two spirits are mingled as one (1 Cor. 6:17)! John 3 does not use the term "Holy Spirit." It only says "the Spirit." The Spirit is mingled with our spirit as one spirit. The Spirit becomes one with man, and this regenerated man becomes one with God. Is this not wonderful? Within us is a part that is mingled with God. God is so high, yet He has become one with us. I feel honored that I am one with God and that I have God one with me. This is the significance of regeneration. I hope all the new believers could have this kind of uplifted understanding regarding regeneration. As soon as we were saved, we became mingled with God.

When we are regenerated, we are made the children of God as the bride of Christ, who is the Bridegroom, for His increase, as typified by Eve as the counterpart to Adam (John 1:12-13; 3:29-30; Gen. 2:21-23). Regeneration makes the believers the children of God. Because we are God's children, we may say that our last name is "God." We all know that our last name is our family name, and we all have become God's family. This is why we call each other brothers and sisters. We are of one Father with one family name.

Individually, we are children of God, but corporately we are one entity, the bride of Christ. In the first part of John 3, the Lord Jesus speaks concerning regeneration. Later in the same chapter, John the Baptist referred to the regenerated ones in totality as the one bride of Christ (John 3:29-30). John seemed to be saying, "I am not the Christ. I am not the one who comes to take the bride. Rather, He is the One, and you who are regenerated are the bride for Him. The One who takes the bride is the Bridegroom, and this Bridegroom has to increase, while I, who am not the Bridegroom, have to be reduced to nothing." Eventually, John the Baptist was reduced to nothing, even to the point of his physical death by being beheaded. When the Lord Jesus was put to death, however, He did not remain in death; He resurrected. In His resurrection, He brought many saved ones with Him and brought them forth to become parts of Him. When all these parts are put together, they become a bride as His counterpart.

The church is the bride of Christ, and according to typology, this bride is typified by Eve, who was Adam's counterpart. Eve was first a part of Adam. While Adam was sleeping, God opened his side and took out a rib. Then God built that rib into a woman by the name of Eve and brought her to Adam to be his counterpart (Gen. 2:21-23). Before this, Adam had given names to all the animals, but he had never found his counterpart. When he saw Eve, he declared, "This is now bone of my bones, and flesh of my flesh" (Gen. 2:23). Eve is a picture of the church. The church came out of Christ as a part of Christ. The intrinsic essence of the church is the incarnated, crucified, and resurrected Christ. He is the essence of the church because the church was His part. The church is not only composed of children born of God, but the church is also the bride, the counterpart of Christ, a part of Christ as Christ's increase.

Before Eve came into existence, she was a rib of Adam, a part of Adam. According to this revelation, we can say that before the church came into existence, she was a part of

Christ. We may feel that this is too deep and beyond our comprehension, but even our physical body created by God is a wonder that we cannot comprehend. We should not trust in our mere mental comprehension of things. We need a revelation of the divine facts. The fact is that the church was a part of Christ before she came into existence. This is why every believer is a member of the Body of Christ. Just as the members of our physical body are parts of us, the members of Christ are parts of Christ. The divine life, the incarnated, crucified, and resurrected Christ Himself, is the essence of the church.

Through the Release of the Divine Life by Christ as the One Grain of Wheat Falling into the Ground and Dying There for His Multiplication

Christ became the essence of the church through the release of the divine life. This divine life had to be released from His Divine Being. If the divine life had only remained in His Divine Being, concealed in His human body, it could have never been our life. For this life to be yours and mine, it had to be released. The divine life was released by Christ as the one grain of wheat falling into the ground and dying there for His multiplication (John 12:24). The life of a grain of wheat is confined within the shell of the grain. When the grain falls into the earth and dies, the shell is broken and the inner life of the grain is released. Christ went through such a death. He was like a grain of wheat falling into the earth and dying in order to be released. With His death, the divine life was released from one grain into many grains.

Through the Impartation of the Divine Life by Christ as the Firstborn Son of God in His Resurrection, That God May Have Many Sons as the Many Brothers of Christ

We were made the children of God as the bride of Christ through the impartation of the divine life by Christ, as the firstborn Son of God in His resurrection, that God may have many sons as the many brothers of Christ (1 Pet. 1:3; Rom. 8:29; Heb. 2:11-12). The release of the divine life is one thing, but the impartation of the divine life is another. The divine life was released out of Christ's human shell. Now this released divine life has been imparted into us, the believers of Christ. This took place at the time Christ was resurrected. His resurrection included us (Eph. 2:6). We all were resurrected in Him, with Him, and by Him. Before we were born, we had already been resurrected nearly two thousand years ago (1 Pet. 1:3). The church is a resurrected item. Before resurrection, God had only one Son, His only begotten Son (John 1:18; 3:16). In His resurrection, He became the firstborn Son with many brothers. Now He is our big Brother, and we are the many sons of God. The divine life imparted into us in Christ's resurrection is the intrinsic essence of the church, the organic Body of Christ.

The Many Brothers of Christ Being
His Many Branches Grafted into Him,
the True Vine in the Universe, to Bear Much Fruit
for His Enlargement in His Spreading, That They
Might Express the Triune God as His Organism

The many brothers of Christ are His many branches grafted into Him, the true vine in the universe, to bear much fruit for His enlargement in His spreading, that they might express the Triune God as His organism (John 15:1, 5, 16, 8). This universal vine tree is our essence. God is our essence, Christ is our essence, and the vine tree is also our essence. The vine tree with its branches, the intrinsic and organic spreading of Christ, becomes Christ's enlargement. In London, England, there is a vine tree which is called the Queen's vine. Someone took me to see this vine tree in 1958. When he remarked about how large this vine was, I replied that this vine did not surprise me because I had seen a much bigger one. I am a branch of that big vine. The Queen's vine is very small in comparison to the true vine. The vine of which I am a part is so long that it encircles the whole earth. This is the real great vine, which is the essence of the church. As the branches of the true vine, we are the multiplication of Christ, the duplication of Christ, the spreading of Christ, and the enlargement of Christ. This multiplication, duplication, spreading, and enlargement, the true vine with its branches, is the organism of the Triune God.

This Organism of the Triune God Being the Organic Body of Christ, Constituted with His Many Brothers as the Many Members of His Organic Body

This organism of the Triune God is the organic Body of Christ constituted with His many brothers as the many members of His organic Body (Eph. 1:22-23; Rom. 12:5). The intrinsic essence of the church as the organic Body of Christ is the Triune God. It is by this intrinsic essence that the church can be held together as one. Our oneness is not in agreeing with one another's doctrines. Our oneness is the processed and dispensing Triune God. Hallelujah for this oneness! If we have any problems with one another, it is because we have departed from the intrinsic essence, the processed and dispensing Triune God. If we stay with Him, forgetting all the different doctrines, there will be no problems.

THE ORGANIC EXISTENCE OF THE CHURCH

Existing in the Universe as the One Universal Church of God for His Universal Expression, the Fullness of God

The church exists in the universe as the one universal church of God for His universal expression, the fullness of God (1 Cor. 10:32; 12:28; Eph. 3:19b). Even the existence of the church is organic. Where the Triune God is, this living, organic church is, because this church is now one with the processed and dispensing Triune God. The church and the processed and dispensing Triune God are not two entities; they have become one entity. It is impossible for such a church to be divided.

Spreading in Many Localities on the Earth as Many Local Churches to Be His Local Expressions

The church is spreading in many localities on the earth as

many local churches to be His local expressions (Rev. 1:4a; 11). Universally, the church exists in the universe. Locally, this church is expressed in many localities as local churches. To say that all the local expressions should be different from one another is a wrong teaching. This kind of erroneous teaching comes from not seeing that the churches are organic, with an intrinsic essence. Does the church in Anaheim have a particular, intrinsic essence different from the church in another locality? This is impossible! In the time of Peter and Paul, every local church had the same one intrinsic essence. All the local churches on the earth today also have only one intrinsic essence, so the church cannot be divided, or split.

Not only the universal church but also the local churches are one. They are intrinsically one in the processed and dispensing Triune God. To solve our problems today, we must come back to the intrinsic essence of the church. If today we all limit ourselves to the one intrinsic essence of the church, every problem will be solved. To talk about whether all the churches are one or separate is to talk in darkness. This is talk without a vision of the intrinsic essence of the church. This chapter should be used by the Lord to "open the window" for us to look into and see the very intrinsic essence of the church and all the churches.

In 1 Corinthians 12:28 Paul says, "And God has placed some in the church: firstly apostles, secondly prophets, thirdly teachers; then works of power, then gifts of healing, helps, administrations, various kinds of tongues." First, God placed the apostles, who are universal in function. Second, He placed the prophets, who are not just universal in function because prophets were a part of the church in Antioch (Acts 13:1). Third, He placed teachers, who were also present locally in Antioch (Acts 13:1). "Helps" refers to the serving ones, the deacons, who help the saints in a local church, and "administrations" refers to the management of the elders in a local church. In 1 Corinthians 12:28, Paul puts apostles (who are universal), prophets and teachers (who are both universal and local), and deacons and elders (who are local) all together. This means the word "church" in this verse implies the universal church and all the local churches.

In the eyes of God, the universal church and all the local churches are just "the church." The processed and now-dispensing Triune God is one, and He is the very essence of the church. Therefore, this church, in both its universal and local aspects, is one church. When we come back to the intrinsic essence of the church, we will not talk wrongly about the differences of the churches. All the churches are the unique, one organism of the processed and dispensing Triune God.

CHAPTER TWO

THE INTRINSIC GROWTH OF THE CHURCH FOR ITS ORGANIC INCREASE

Scripture Reading: 1 Pet. 2:2; Heb. 5:12-14; 1 Cor. 3:6b; Col. 2:19; 1:28; Eph. 4:13b; John 3:29-30a; 15:1, 5, 8; Eph. 4:16

OUTLINE

I. The intrinsic growth of the church:
   A. Through the feeding on the guileless milk and the solid food of the word by the members of Christ—1 Pet. 2:2; Heb. 5:12-14.
   B. Through the watering on the Body of Christ by its gifted members—1 Cor. 3:6b.
   C. Through the giving of growth in life to the members of Christ by God—1 Cor. 3:6c.
   D. By God's growing in the believers—Col. 2:19.
   E. Unto maturity in the divine life—Col. 1:28; Eph. 4:13b.
   F. Reaching the measure of the stature of the fullness of Christ—the organic Body of Christ—Eph. 4:13c.

II. The organic increase of the church:
   A. The increase of Christ in His organic Body as His bride—John 3:29-30a.
   B. The increase of God in the growth of life within the members of the organic Body of Christ—Col. 2:19.
   C. The multiplication of Christ in the fruit-bearing by the branches of Christ, the true vine in the universe, as the organism of the Triune God—John 15:1, 5, 8.

D. The growth of the organic Body of Christ, with the divine life as the growing element, for the organic building up of the Body of Christ—Eph. 4:16.

1 Peter 2:2   intensly yearn for
As newborn babes, long for the guileless milk of the word in

Eph 1-13 Fullness of Christ Church's highest definition

~~John 3:9~~

Need:
- intrinsically, inwardly need= grow in life
- Outwardly = bear fruits.

(organic, intrinsic grow)
3 substances of power =
Prayer. Spirit. and the word.

Education. Virtues. → Christian IBM. Christian Google. | Worldly method | v.s. | No much prayer |
                                                          | - Clever gimmicks |

What are you reproducing? We reproduce what we are.

We need an organism (require divine life), rather than an ~~organism~~ Organization (natural talent, capability.)

                        of Christ
enjoyment of riches, or ~~to~~ by human endeavor?
new churches raised by

What's your source? Who is your head!

Apart from the divine life.

Is this organic? Is this intrinsic?
Sth matches Him intrinsically & organically.

THE INTRINSIC GROWTH OF THE CHURCH
FOR ITS ORGANIC INCREASE

In the last chapter, we saw the intrinsic essence of the church for its organic existence. Now we want to see the intrinsic growth of the church for its organic increase. The essence is for existence, and the growth is for increase. A child is organic, something of life, and its beginning is at birth. Following birth, every child's greatest need is growth. The church is also something organic, full of life. It is not an organization, void of life. We should forget about the common concept of the church as an organization or some social body. It is true that the church is a corporate entity, but it is not something organized. It is something born.

The Bible calls this birth regeneration. Paul was regenerated over nineteen hundred years ago, and I was regenerated just about sixty-four years ago. Everyone who believes in the Lord was regenerated at some point in time. However, in God's sight we all were regenerated at the same time. First Peter 1:3 says, "Blessed be the God and Father of our Lord Jesus Christ, who according to His great mercy has regenerated us unto a living hope through the resurrection of Jesus Christ from among the dead." This is a crucial verse. It tells us God *has* regenerated all His chosen people. We were not regenerated separately. According to 1 Peter 1:3 we all were regenerated at the time the Lord Jesus was resurrected. We have been regenerated *through* His resurrection.

All the countless believers, regardless of how many millions there are, are as one man in the sight of God. This universal man is the new man (Eph. 2:15). The Head of this new man is Christ, and the Body of this new man is the church. The church is the Body of Christ. This is not the individual Christ, but the corporate Christ, the enlarged Christ.

THE INTRINSIC GROWTH OF THE CHURCH

The essence of the church is the divine life which is the processed and dispensing Triune God. We all have been regenerated with this divine life. The church is now growing in this life, by this life, with this life, and through this life. The growth of the church is its intrinsic growth, its organic growth. This organic growth has nothing to do with organization.

Through the Feeding on the Guileless Milk and the Solid Food of the Word by the Members of Christ

The intrinsic growth of the church is through the feeding on the guileless milk and the solid food of the word by the members of Christ (1 Pet. 2:2; Heb. 5:12-14). An infant does not grow by self-effort. He does not grow by stretching out his feet and crying, "Let me grow!" He grows by eating. The more he eats, the more he grows. One of my grandchildren was very small at birth and had to be sustained by the use of an incubator. Today, however, he is a strong, big boy because he has been eating all these years. He has been taking in all the rich, nourishing American food. He has been drinking milk and eating all the rich produce of America.

As members of the Body of Christ, we should drink the guileless milk of the word that we may grow. Then we must eat the solid food of the word so that we may grow even more. Our eating of the word causes us to grow in a strong way. The Word is full of food, but some only get knowledge according to the letter when they read the Bible. This is a shame because the sixty-six books of the Bible are a menu of Christ. Christ is our real food and every page of the Bible is a description of this rich Christ. He is either expressed or implied throughout the whole Bible. Actually, the implied Christ is richer and more nourishing than the expressed Christ. When we come to the Bible, we should come with a seeking heart after Christ. We should pray, "Lord, I come to Your Word. I do not care for teachings alone, but I care for You. Lord, feed me with Yourself through this Word." We all should have such a prayer.

The Bible is full of Christ. Without Christ, this book becomes empty. The Bible is like a peanut shell. It contains Christ as its kernel. Without Christ, the Bible is like an empty shell. If we have a heart toward Christ, He will nourish us with Himself when we come to the Word. When we come to the Bible, we must have the full faith that God exists and that

He is a rewarder of those who seek Him out (Heb. 11:6). In the whole universe the most wonderful One is God. He is Spirit; He is invisible, yet so real (John 4:24), and He is the content of the Bible.

I have studied the Bible for more than sixty years. I have also studied world history, and I have been observing the world situation very closely all these years. As a serious student of the Bible, I have come to understand many of the prophecies concerning the history of the world, including many things that are presently occurring. I have seen many of the biblical prophecies fulfilled in my lifetime. The fulfillment of these prophecies shows how wonderful and marvelous the Bible is.

When I was a young man of about nineteen in 1925, I found out about the prophecy in the Bible that the nation of Israel would be restored (Matt. 24:32). I knew that the Jews had lost their homeland and that they were scattered throughout the earth. They were dispersed and scattered to such an extent that they had become citizens of many different countries. I believed the Word of God, but still in my mind there was a question. How could such a race be recovered to become a nation once more? This seemed to be impossible, yet the Bible clearly indicated that this would happen. In 1948, forty-one years ago, I was working in Shanghai when the news said that the nation of Israel had been restored. I was very excited when I heard this news because I knew that it was a fulfillment of the Lord's prophecy.

The Bible also prophesied in Luke 21:24 that the city of Jerusalem would eventually be returned to the people of Israel. Jerusalem was taken over by the king of Babylon, Nebuchadnezzar, about twenty-six centuries ago, in approximately 600 B.C. The Lord Jesus prophesied in Luke 21:24 that "Jerusalem will be trampled by the nations until the times of the Gentiles are fulfilled." From the time of Nebuchadnezzar, Jerusalem was trodden under the feet of the Gentiles throughout the centuries. I wondered how it would be possible for the Jews to regain Jerusalem. Nineteen years after the nation of Israel had been restored, in 1967, the city of Jerusalem was reclaimed by the Jews. This was a

wonderful fulfillment of biblical prophecy. When I heard this
news, I was greatly excited, for I knew the prophecy in Luke
21:24.

Another wonderful fulfillment of prophecy can be seen in
the interpretation of the image in Daniel 2, which was a part
of King Nebuchadnezzar's dream. Daniel's interpretation of
this image is actually a prophecy concerning the nations
of the earth. Daniel 2:31-34 says, "Thou, O king, sawest, and
behold, a great image. This great image, which was mighty,
and whose brightness was excellent, stood before thee; and
the aspect thereof was terrible. As for this image, its head was
of fine gold, its breast and its arms of silver, its belly and its
thighs of brass, its legs of iron, its feet part of iron, and part of
clay" (ASV).

All biblical students who are familiar with prophecy know
that the image illustrates the world political situation beginning with Nebuchadnezzar. The head of gold symbolizes
Nebuchadnezzar, the king of Babylon, and thus the Babylonian
Empire (vv. 37-38). The breast and arms of silver symbolize
Medo-Persia (v. 39). The belly and thighs of bronze symbol-
ize the empire of Macedonia and Greece under Alexander
the Great (v. 39). Following the Greek Empire, is the Roman
Empire (v. 40). It is symbolized by the two legs of iron, indi-
cating its tremendous strength. The two legs signify that the
Roman Empire was divided into two parts, the eastern Roman
Empire and the western Roman Empire.

The four kingdoms are symbolized by gold, silver, brass,
and iron. The first is gold, indicating that its beginning is
more glorious. The glory reduces with each succeeding metal,
yet it remains very strong. Finally, the feet of the image are
part iron and part clay signifying the nations in the period
after the fall of Rome and before the second coming of Christ.
Th‎‎‎‎‎ would be part autocracy and part democracy.

ly part of this century, communism crept into
. The Soviet revolution occurred in 1917. After
communism took control in China. The philoso-
inism was their boast. Actually, they simply
itorship, or autocracy. Today it has been about
rom the time communism had its beginnings in

Russia. Communism is like the iron in the feet of the image. It is strong to crush whatever stands in its way, but God has a way to weaken the iron. His way is to mix it with clay. In these days the people of eastern Europe, who are the clay, the dust, are rising up to deal with and weaken the iron of communism. Eventually, the iron cannot deal with the dust, and it becomes paralyzed, crippled. This demonstrates the fulfillment of prophecy in eastern Europe, and that we are in the iron-clay stage of the image. Millions are rising up in eastern Europe. Recently, millions rose up in Red China in a desire for freedom. As the clay rises up, the strength of the iron is weakened.

At the end of Nebuchadnezzar's dream, a stone, cut out without hands, smote the image upon its feet, which were of iron and clay, and broke them to pieces (Dan. 2:34). This is a prophecy concerning Christ. He is the stone, cut out without human hands, which will come down from heaven to smite the image, the kingdoms of the earth, and break them into pieces. Then He will become a great mountain, the kingdom of God, which will fill the whole earth (Dan. 2:35; Rev. 11:15).

Whatever is recorded in the Bible is eventually related to Christ. Even when we read these prophecies, we can find nourishment. Christ, as the content of the Bible, is food to us. The Bible is a book inspired by God. This means that any time we come to the Bible with a seeking heart, the Spirit of God will be with us.

The Triune God is involved with the Bible. This is why this book is so unique. I recall a story that occurred in the past century. An unbelieving American citizen was visiting a country in Latin America and observed a native of that country sitting and reading a Bible. The American began to ridicule that person because he was reading the Bible. That native had been a cannibal before being saved, and he responded in this way: "Sir, if this Bible had not gotten into me, you would have been inside of me already." His eating the Word of God had transformed him, and he was no longer a wild cannibal. Only the Bible could do this!

There are many cases of people being changed just by reading one portion of the Bible. This was the situation with one brother who eventually became a co-worker among us. When he was young, he was a very patriotic, active, and capable nationalist. He hated the foreign countries and their foreign religion, Christianity. One day, he went sightseeing to a certain mountain and entered an idol temple. To his surprise, someone had left a large Bible there. It had been there for a long time because it was covered with dust. This Bible was opened to Psalm 1. He began to read Psalm 1 out of curiosity. As he read, he thought, "Is this what is in the Bible?" As he read on and on, he eventually began to weep, and rolled on the ground repenting. Reading the Bible caused him to get saved. He was changed to such an extent that he decided to drop his political associations and become a follower of Christ. He became burdened to take the Bible throughout China in order to preach the gospel of Christ. He told this to me personally, and he later became one of our co-workers. This shows the effectiveness and wonder of the Bible!

Many Christians can testify that the Bible has had such a wonderful impact on their lives. For us to grow, we need the milk and the solid food that is in this book. If we do not eat physical food for a period of time, we will starve and eventually die. If we do not read the Bible for a whole week, we will starve spiritually. When we read this book with a desire to seek after Christ, we will be fed. Thousands of Christians can testify that when they read the Bible, they do not receive mere knowledge according to the letter, but they get Christ into them. This Christ, as the life-giving Spirit, is food to us (John 6:57; 1 Cor. 15:45b). As the life-giving Spirit, He is dispensing Himself into us and supplying us with Himself as life.

When we open any page of the Bible, we should read with a seeking heart and pray, "Lord, I love You, so I come to Your Word. Be my drink and be my food." When we pray in this way, we will realize that Christ, who is now the life-giving Spirit, is within us dispensing Himself and supplying us with Himself as our food. This supply of life will cause us to grow. I believe we all can testify to this. This is the wonder of the Bible. It is not just a book. It is a book filled with Christ. It is a book in which our God is fully involved. When we touch this book with a seeking heart for Christ, we touch the Spirit, we receive the very life-giving Christ, and we grow organically.

Through the Watering on the Body of Christ
by Its Gifted Members

The church grows through eating, and also through the watering on the Body of Christ by its gifted members (1 Cor. 3:6). We believers are living plants who have been planted into Christ (1 Cor. 3:6a, 9b). Christ is our good ground, our earth. He is the rich soil into which we have been planted and in which we grow. Once a plant has been planted, it needs to be watered. Southern California used to be very dry with very little plant life. Then southern California began to receive water from the state of Nevada, and the result is that it has become very green and beautiful. The sprinklers in many yards in southern California water the lawns to keep them green and growing. In a spiritual sense, we need such watering so that we may grow. Paul said, "I planted, Apollos watered" (1 Cor. 3:6a). We need the watering by the gifted persons. For our spiritual growth, we need the food that the Word provides, and we also need the watering that the gifted ones provide. *Thomas missed a meeting he missed resurrected Christ.*

If you are in the meetings of the church, you will be blessed with much watering. Regardless of how much time you spend reading the Bible in your home, it cannot replace the meetings of the church. Some saints may become unhappy with the elders or with some brother or sister in the church. They may reason, "I do not need to go to the church meetings. I have the Bible, so I will stay home and read my Bible. The Lord is omnipresent, so I will dedicate the meeting time to stay at home and read my Bible for two hours." However, they will find that such an attempt leaves them short of the great benefit received in the church meetings.

You may say that you do not like the meeting, but whether you like the meeting or not, the "sprinklers" are there "sprinkling." Regardless of how much you endeavor to get something in your home away from the meeting, there is no "sprinkler" watering you in your home. The church meeting may not seem so good to you, but you will still be watered in the meeting. Sometimes some saints may sleep in the meeting, but they still experience the watering.

In the meetings of the church, we are always dealing with the Bible. As we have fellowshipped, God the Spirit is totally involved with this book. When we go to the meetings of the church, we are always touching His Word, so we are always receiving something of God. Some have said to me, "Brother Lee, you should not ask the saints to read so many verses. It seems that sometimes there are fifty verses." I responded that even fifty verses is not that many. Psalm 119 has one hundred seventy-six verses. It would be wonderful if we could read this entire psalm in some meeting. Years ago, when the saints were still meeting at Elden Hall in Los Angeles, they came together for a prayer meeting and pray-read the entire book of Ephesians. The saints who were in that meeting testified how wonderful it was. When we are in the meetings of the church, we get thoroughly watered because we are under the "sprinkling," the watering.

The gifted members of the Body of Christ, the servants of God, are like the sprinklers on the lawns; they have the ability to sprinkle us with water. The more they talk to us about the Bible, the more they sprinkle us with water. We can testify that when we come to a ministry meeting and listen to the speaking of the gifted persons with all the Bible verses, we can never be the same. Whether or not we understand everything, we always go away from such meetings with the water of the Bible. I do not have much knowledge in fields other than the Bible, but by the Lord's mercy, I somewhat know this holy book. I can open this book and water the saints. My speaking in the ministry of God's word is the sprinkling. We need to come to the meetings of the church and of the ministry to take a "shower" or a "bath" in the water of the word.

Through the Giving of Growth in Life
to the Members of Christ by God

The intrinsic growth of the church is through the giving of growth in life to the members of Christ by God (1 Cor. 3:6c). The gifted ones may do the planting and the watering, but it is God who gives the growth in life. This is why I must always take some time to pray before I come to speak in a meeting. I pray that the Lord would be one with me and infuse me with

Himself so that whatever I speak would be in Him. I believe He has richly answered these prayers because quite often, as I am speaking, I feel supplied within to speak with new light and instant utterance.

We need the feeding from the Bible directly, and we need the watering from the ones who know the Bible more. God goes along with our reading of the Word and with the speaking of the gifted members to give us the growth. The feeding and the watering are the top means used by Him to give His life to us. When we get into the Word, we are feeding. When we get under the speaking of the word, we receive the watering. Then God gives the growth.

By God's Growing in the Believers

The intrinsic growth of the church is by God's growing in the believers (Col. 2:19). We were reborn by the divine life, which is God Himself. Now we are being fed and watered, and God is causing us to grow. This growth is God Himself growing in us (Col. 2:19). When God gives us the growth in life, this means that He is increasing Himself within us. As we are feeding on the Word, and as we are being watered by the gifted ones, God Himself is moving and growing within us.

The last part of Colossians 2:19 tells us that the Body "grows with the growth of God." We grow by God's growing within us. Of course, God in Himself is not growing because He is complete and perfect. His growing is within us, and how much He grows within us depends upon how much room we will give to Him to grow. We may be full of the world, of ourselves, of our own interests, but by reading the Bible, little by little the word of the Bible takes away some part of our worldliness, some part of our self-interest, and some part of our love for things other than God Himself. Then within us more room is given to God. Then He takes this room and expands and increases within us. This increase is His growth in us. His growth becomes our growth because we and He are one. The growth of the church is God's growth in the church. By our feeding on the Word and being watered by the gifted members, the negative things within us are taken away and there is more room for the very God who dwells in us. When

Growth in life unto maturity ──→ Body ──→ Bride
  (eating & drinking)
Obedience to the Lord by eating the obedient one.

32   THE ORGANIC BUILDING UP OF THE CHURCH

He gets more room, He grows within us. This issues in the church's organic growth.

Unto Maturity in the Divine Life, Reaching the Measure of the Stature of the Fullness of Christ—the Organic Body of Christ

God's growth in us is unto our maturity in the divine life (Col. 1:28; Eph. 4:13b). As we are growing, we are maturing until we reach the measure of the stature of the fullness of Christ (Eph. 4:13c). The fullness of Christ is the organic Body of Christ (Eph. 1:23); thus, the measure of the stature of the fullness of Christ is the measure of the stature of the Body of Christ. Christ fills all in all, and He needs a great Body as His fullness. The Body of Christ, which is His expression, has a stature and this stature has a measure. The church grows with the growth of God until it reaches maturity. When it reaches maturity, it arrives at the measure of the stature of the fullness of Christ (Eph. 4:13). By then the church will be Christ's expression in full. This is the highest peak of the church's growth.

THE ORGANIC INCREASE OF THE CHURCH

The Increase of Christ in His Organic Body as His Bride

The church grows until it reaches maturity, which is the measure of the stature of the Body of Christ for His expression. This growth is for the organic increase of the church. This organic increase is the increase of Christ in His organic Body as His bride (John 3:29-30a). The fullness of Christ is His Body, and the Body of Christ is His counterpart, His bride. This is based upon the type of Eve being the counterpart of Adam.

God in His wisdom did not create a couple, but a single man, a "bachelor." God brought all the living creatures to Adam and Adam gave names to all of them, but among these Adam did not find his counterpart. Finally, God put Adam to sleep, opened his side, and took out a rib. In typology, this is a picture of what happened to Christ in His death. His death on the cross was His being "put to sleep" by God. In the Bible, sleep means death (1 Cor. 15:18; 1 Thes. 4:13-16; John 11:11-14). When Christ was sleeping on the cross, a soldier pierced His side and out came blood and water (John 19:34). All that came out of Adam's side was the rib without the blood. At Adam's time in Genesis 2 there was no sin, so there was no need of blood for redemption. When Christ was sleeping on the cross, however, there was the problem of sin, so His death had to deal first with this sin problem. The blood came out of Christ's side for redemption. Following the blood, the water came out. The rib taken out of Adam's side and the water that flowed out of the side of Christ at the cross both signify the divine life. God used this rib, which was a part of Adam, and built a woman to be Adam's counterpart. Now God builds up the church with the divine life, the resurrection life of Christ.

Eve was built to match Adam in his image and likeness. When God brought Eve to Adam, he said, "This is now bone of my bones, and flesh of my flesh" (Gen. 2:23). Eve became the counterpart of Adam and the increase of Adam. The man is not complete without the woman. The wife is the other half of the man, making him complete and being his increase. The church as the bride of Christ is the increase of Christ, the Bridegroom. This is clearly revealed in John 3:29-30, "He who has the bride is the bridegroom; but the friend of the bridegroom, who stands and hears him, rejoices with joy because of the bridegroom's voice. This joy of mine therefore is made full. He must increase, but I must decrease." John the Baptist was saying that the bride is for the Bridegroom and the Bridegroom is increasing. He, John the Baptist, should not be considered because he is decreasing, being reduced to nothing. All our attention should be focused on the increasing Christ, who is now increasing all over the earth.

The Increase of God in the Growth of Life within the Members of the Organic Body of Christ

Christ is increasing, and God is increasing in the growth of life within the members of the organic Body of Christ. Colossians 2:19 says, "Holding the Head, out from whom all the Body, by means of the joints and bands being supplied and knit together, grows with the growth of God." To grow is a matter of life, which is God Himself. As the Body of Christ, the church should not be deprived of Christ, who is the embodiment of God (Col. 2:9) as the source of life. By holding Christ, the Head, the church grows with the growth of God, with the increase of God as life.

The Multiplication of Christ in the Fruit-bearing by the Branches of Christ, the True Vine in the Universe, as the Organism of the Triune God

The organic increase of the church is the multiplication of Christ in the fruit-bearing by the branches of Christ, the true vine in the universe, as the organism of the Triune God (John 15:1, 5, 8). All the Christians are the duplication and the multiplication of Christ. We, as the many grains, are a multiplication of Christ, as the one grain, which fell into the earth to die (John 12:24). This multiplication of Christ is in the fruit-bearing by the branches of Christ. As His branches, we must go forth to bear fruit. The Lord Jesus said that He appointed us to go forth to bear fruit and that our fruit should remain (John 15:16). The fruit borne by us is the multiplication of the vine tree.

The vine tree with all its branches and all its fruit is the organism of the Triune God. The Triune God in His organism is the focus of chapters fourteen through sixteen of the Gospel of John. This organism is the increase of the church. As branches of this divine organism, we have to live an increasing life, which is a fruit-bearing life. If we say that we enjoy Christ and abide in Christ according to John 15, we must be bearing fruit. If we are not bearing fruit and we say that we are abiding in Christ, we are deceiving ourselves. Genuine abiding in Christ will cause us to bear fruit. Our enjoyment is vain if we are not bearing fruit. We are branches, and the duty and responsibility of the branches is fruit-bearing. The fruit borne by the branches is the multiplication and the duplication of the vine tree. The increase of the vine tree is the increase of Christ, and the increase of Christ is the increase of the church.

The Growth of the Organic Body of Christ, with the Divine Life as the Growing Element, for the Organic Building Up of the Body of Christ

The organic increase of the church is the growth of the organic Body of Christ, with the divine life as the growing element, for the organic building up of the Body of Christ (Eph. 4:16). In the Body of Christ, there are two categories of members: the joints and each one part. The joints and the parts can be compared to the two categories of materials in a building. The steel beams of this big meeting hall are joined closely together into a steel frame. Then the stones and wood of this building are put together, knit together, by being interwoven. God's building, the Body of Christ, needs to be joined closely together through every joint of the rich supply and knit together through the operation in measure of each one part.

The joints are equal to the gifts mentioned in Ephesians 4:11: "And He gave some apostles, and some prophets, and some evangelists, and some shepherds and teachers." There are many joints in a human body, and a healthy body needs the proper function of all its joints. If a person's fingers did not have joints, his hand could not function properly. A simple task, such as picking up a fork to eat, would be quite awkward. The joints are all necessary so that a person's body can operate normally.

The church, as the Body of Christ, also needs the proper function of all the joints. In the church we need many joints. If a local church has only two or three joints of supply, and these joints are only the elders, that is a poor local church. A proper church will be full of joints. In every church there should be many joints providing the rich supply. The rich supply that the joints supply to the Body is Christ Himself. Ephesians 4:16 says, "Out from whom all the Body, joined closely together and knit together through every joint of the rich supply, and through the operation in measure of each one part, causes the growth of the Body unto the building up of itself in love." This verse speaks of "the rich supply." The use of the definite article "the" indicates that there is a particular supply of Christ that each joint has for the benefit of the Body.

The second category of members in the Body is "each one part." In a person's physical body, there are many parts. The joints do not constitute the whole body, so there is the need for all the parts to match and complement the joints. As the joints in the Body of Christ are supplying, the parts should all be operating. Thank the Lord that every member is useful. This is why we all need to endeavor to pick up the God-ordained way of serving which brings all the members of the Body of Christ into function. This is such a contrast to our old way, which annulled the function of most of the members. Every local church should be full of joints supplying and parts operating. This is accomplished by the intrinsic growth. If we are growing in the divine life, in the divine Trinity, we will not be useless. We will be very useful. All of us will be active, living members of the organic Body of Christ.

When the Body of Christ is functioning properly through the active participation of the joints and each one part, "all the Body...causes the growth of the Body unto the building up of itself in love." It is quite marvelous that all the Body causes the Body to grow. In Greek, the word "unto" means "with a view to," "for the purpose of," or "resulting in." The growth of the Body results in the building up of itself in love. This is the intrinsic growth of the church for the church's organic increase, issuing in the organic building up of the Body of Christ.

CHAPTER THREE

THE INTRINSIC BUILDING UP OF THE CHURCH FOR ITS ORGANIC FUNCTION

Scripture Reading: Eph. 4:8-16; 1 Cor. 12:28; Acts 13:1; Rom. 12:4-8; 1 Cor. 12:4-11; 14:4b, 12; Eph. 1:23b

OUTLINE

I. The intrinsic building up of the church:
   A. By the ascended Head giving the gifts—Eph. 4:8-11.
   B. By the Head-given gifts—the apostles, prophets, evangelists, and shepherds and teachers—perfecting the saints—Eph. 4:11-12:
      1. In the local churches—1 Cor. 12:28; Acts 13:1.
      2. Unto the work of the ministry—the building up of the organic Body of Christ—Eph. 4:12.
      3. Until all the members of Christ arrive at:
         a. The oneness of the faith and of the full knowledge of the Son of God.
         b. A full-grown man.
         c. The measure of the stature of the fullness of Christ—the church as the organic Body of Christ—Eph. 4:13.
   C. Through all the perfected members of the Body of Christ—Eph. 4:14-16:
      1. Being no longer babes tossed by waves and carried about by every wind of teaching in the sleight of men, in craftiness with a view to a system of error—v. 14.
      2. But holding to truth in love to grow up into the Head, Christ, in all things—v. 15.

   3. Out from the Head—v. 16a.
   4. All the Body, joined closely together through
      every joint of the rich supply, and knit together
      through the operation in measure of each part,
      causing the growth of the Body unto the build-
      ing up of itself in love—v. 16b.
II. The organic function of the church:
   A. In the organic Body of Christ—Rom. 12:4-8.
   B. In the local expressions of the organic Body of
      Christ—1 Cor. 12:28.
   C. By the move of the Triune God:
      1. In the operations of God.
      2. Through the ministries of the Lord.
      3. With the gifts of the Spirit in His manifesta-
         tions to the members of the organic Body of
         Christ—1 Cor. 12:4-11.
   D. For the building up of the church as the organic
      Body of Christ, the fullness of the One who fills all
      in all—1 Cor. 14:4b, 12; Eph. 1:23b.

The Intrinsic element of the church: divine life.

THE INTRINSIC BUILDING UP OF THE CHURCH

essential. hidden   Growth is the ~~best~~ need. the building up of the church.

In chapter one we saw the intrinsic essence of the church
for its organic existence. In chapter two we saw the intrinsic
growth of the church for its organic increase. In this chapter
we want to see the intrinsic building up of the church for its
organic function. *then our unique function will be manifested.*

then we can perfect others. that they can grow unto maturity.

A physical building is built by putting together and fitting
together various materials. Such a building, however, is lifeless.
It is not organic. God's building is organic, and the best example
of such an organic building is a living person. A living person
is a real building. God took a rib out of Adam's side and built
that rib into a woman (Gen. 2:21-23). This woman was a building. God created Adam, the husband, but God did not create a
wife. God built up a wife for Adam. The man was created by
God, and the woman was built by God. God's building work is
finer than His creating work. Man, as the one created by God,
is rougher than the female, who was built by God. Males are
rough, and females are fine. A female's face, hands, voice, and
actions are finer than the male's. The female is much finer,
because she was built by God. God built up a woman.

☞ The gifted ones drown replace them. But help them to bring in their function. Romans 12:6 And

All the brothers are males in the old creation, but we are
females in the new creation. In the new creation we are the
bride of Christ; we are God's building. The Body of Christ,
the church, is a bride that was not created, but built up. God's
building, of course, is much finer than a physical building. The
church's building is organic by the growth in life. Because it is
organic, it is intrinsic. Anything that is intrinsic is fine. The
building up of the church is typified by God's fine work
of building a woman for man.

The building up of the church is actually the growth of the
church. Every full-grown person began as a small baby. The
building up of that person over the years was accomplished by
that person's growth. When he ate, he grew, and this growth
was his organic building up. <u>If we mean business to have the
church built up, we must take care of our growth in the divine
life</u>. This means we must be those <u>eating and drinking Christ</u>.
We grow with what we eat, and what we eat becomes our very
constitution. We are what we eat.

function connection growth in life

We must become Christ. → To live is Christ.

Paul with the members (Paul with the Head).

John 12:24 grains

Romans 8:29 the firstborn among many brother → Many identical grains/twins

Genesis 1:26   John 14:20 Philippians 2:5 Let this mind be in you.
and I in you.

40   THE ORGANIC BUILDING UP OF THE CHURCH

We grow by what we eat, and what we eat eventually becomes us. We need to eat more of Christ. Some Cantonese people eat six or seven times a day. How many times do we eat Christ? We need to learn of the Cantonese in our eating of the spiritual food. The more times we eat Christ, the better. The more we eat Christ, the more we grow in Christ, and the more we eat Christ, the more we become Christ. When we eat Christ, we grow by Him. This growing is the building up. Therefore, what is built up is Christ. Eventually, the built-up church is just Christ.

By the Ascended Head Giving the Gifts

The intrinsic building up of the church is by the ascended Head giving the gifts (Eph. 4:8-11). Ephesians 4:8 says, "Wherefore He says, Having ascended to the height, He led captive those taken captive and gave gifts to men." We may appreciate the Lord's coming down from the heavens, but we also need an uplifted appreciation of His ascension. In Ephesians 4:8, Paul points out that it is the ascended Christ who is able to give the gifts.

When Paul said that Christ "ascended to the height," he quoted from Psalm 68:18. "Height" in this verse refers to Mount Zion (Psa. 68:15-16), symbolizing the third heaven, where God dwells (1 Kings 8:30). Psalm 68 implies that it was in the ark that God ascended to Mount Zion after the ark had won the victory. Verse 1 of Psalm 68 is a quotation of Numbers 10:35. It indicates that the background of Psalm 68 is God's move in the tabernacle with the ark as its center. Wherever the ark, a type of Christ, went, the victory was won. Eventually, this ark ascended triumphantly to the top of Mount Zion. This portrays how Christ has won the victory and ascended triumphantly to the heavens.

In His ascension, Christ "led captive those taken captive." The redeemed saints had been taken captive by Satan before being saved by Christ's death and resurrection. We were captives under Satan's hand through sin and death. But Christ defeated Satan, solved the problem of sin and death, and rescued us out of the hand of Satan. Then He led us to the heavens as His captives. He took these captives and made them gifts to men.

One of these gifts was Saul of Tarsus, who later became Paul, the apostle. He had been a captive of Satan and a top sinner. In 1 Timothy 1:15 Paul said that he was "the foremost" sinner. He was a big captive of Satan under sin and death, but one day Christ rescued him. He was on the way to Damascus to arrest those who called on the Lord's name (Acts 9:1-2, 14). Then the Lord Jesus seized him and rescued him out of the hand of Satan. Saul was Satan's captive, but he became Christ's captive.

Saul of Tarsus had been opposing Christ and devastating the church. Suddenly he became a gift. Christ took this one and made him a gift by the name of Paul. He became a gift who could expound the Old Testament, who could preach the gospel, teach the saints, and prophesy. How could Paul become such a gift? He himself tells us with a parenthetical word in Ephesians 4:9-10: "Now this, He ascended, what is it except that He also descended into the lower parts of the earth? He who descended is the same who also ascended far above all the heavens that He might fill all things."

Paul was a wonderful writer. He wrote this portion in describing Christ's death and resurrection to accomplish His full redemption and impart life to us. Christ first descended to the earth from the heavenly throne in the third heavens. He did this through the process of incarnation. He lived on the earth for thirty-three and a half years. Then He entered into death, and in death He descended further. In the second step of His descension, He descended into the lower parts of the earth. This refers to Hades, underneath the earth, where Christ went after His death (Acts 2:27). The first step of Christ's descension was for His incarnation. The second step was for His redemption. His descension was the means to accomplish His all-inclusive, full redemption, which has saved us from sin, death, Satan, and the lake of fire. In the first step of His ascension, He ascended from Hades to the earth in resurrection. In His resurrection He imparted life into us. His descension accomplished redemption, and His ascension accomplished the impartation of life. In the second step of His ascension, He brought us to the Father in the third heavens.

When He ascended before His disciples into heaven (Luke 24:51; Acts 1:9-11), they did not fully understand what was going on. They only saw Jesus ascending. But the Scriptures reveal that when Jesus was ascending, He was ascending with a train of vanquished foes. The Amplified New Testament renders "He led a train of vanquished foes" for "He led captive those taken captive." When He was ascending, He was a returning General who had won the victory over Satan, sin, and death. He defeated all of His enemies, and He had many captives. He brought these captives with Him in a procession to celebrate His victory.

Peter and John did not see this when the Lord ascended before their eyes, but the angels saw a tremendous and great train of vanquished foes as a procession for the celebration of Christ's victory. We were there in that procession; Satan was there; and death was also there. What a procession that was! The Lord then presented us, the redeemed saints, His defeated and vanquished foes, as a present to the Father. It is as though He said, "Father, here are the persons You have given to Me. They were dead captives of Satan. Now I have captured them; I rescued them out of the hand of Satan, out from under sin and death. I have also imparted My life into them through My resurrection, the first step of My ascension from Hades to the earth. Now they are not dead, but living presents. I give them all to You as a big, corporate present."

This present included all of the redeemed saints. It included Peter, Paul, Martin Luther, John Nelson Darby, and Watchman Nee. I am honored to be included in this present. We were all included there in Christ's ascension as a big, living present to the Father. The Father, no doubt, was so happy. He could have said, "I am so happy for My redeemed people. They were dead and captured by Satan. But My Son, through His death and resurrection, rescued them and imparted life into them, making them living."

We all must realize that we have already been to the heavens. We were there with Christ, because He brought us, as His present, to the Father. He did not go empty-handed. He went to the Father with all His redeemed ones, including you and me, as a corporate present to the Father. The Father then gave us back to the Son as gifts for His Body (Psa. 68:18). Thus, through His descension and ascension, Christ rescued us, enlivened us, and made us gifts with His resurrection life.

Paul was such a gift. Sometimes I have wondered how Paul received such great revelations, such as the revelation in Ephesians 4. Undoubtedly, Christ spent some particular time with Paul. After he was saved, Paul went to Arabia and stayed there for a period of time (Gal. 1:17). No one knows what he did there, but, no doubt, during this time there was much contact between him and Christ. I believe the Lord used this time to constitute Paul into a big gift to His Body. When Paul returned from Arabia, he was able to preach and to speak wonderful things. That means he became a big gift to the church in the category of the gifted persons mentioned in Ephesians 4:11. This is why he was able to describe Christ's death and resurrection in the marvelous way of verses 8 through 10.

We all should learn to preach the gospel in such a rich way as that portrayed in Ephesians 4. We may speak in this way to our unbelieving contacts: "I would like to tell you that our Savior descended in two steps. He descended from the heavens to the earth and then from the earth to Hades. In the first step of His descension, He accomplished incarnation; He became a man. In the second step of His descension, He entered into death and even went into Hades, dying for us to save us from sin, death, and Satan. As sinners, we were captives of Satan, but through the death of Christ we were forgiven and even rescued from Satan. Then the Lord ascended from Hades to the earth in resurrection. In His resurrection He imparted Himself into us as life. He accomplished redemption through His death and life-impartation through His resurrection. Then we were made alive. In the second step of His ascension, He led us as a train of vanquished foes to the third heaven to give us as a present to His Father." Sometimes we should preach the gospel in this way when we go out to visit people.

During the time of the Roman Empire, when a general gained a victory, all his captives became a procession in the celebration of his victory. Eventually, some of these captives were put to death, and some were given life (2 Cor. 2:15-16). The ones in this procession who were put to death were Satan and his fallen angels, and the ones who were made alive were us, the redeemed saints. After we were presented to the Father as a present and the Father gave us back to the Son as gifts, the Son gave us all as gifts to His Body for its building up.

Every saint, great and small, is a gift to the church. Every member of the Body is a gift to the Body. We may be only a small member, like the little finger, but still we are very necessary. My little finger works so well to comfort my ear when I have an itch inside of it. We should never consider ourselves as too small to be a profitable gift to the Body. The practice of Christianity with one man speaking and the others listening spoils the gifts and kills the functions of the saints. Some Christians in the denominations do not even know how to pray because their function has been annulled by the clergy-laity system. In this system, only the trained "professionals" learn how to function while the rest are laymen. There is a Chinese proverb which says, "If you are sick, go to a doctor. If you have a lawsuit, go to a lawyer. If you want to pray, go to a pastor." According to the biblical revelation, however, all the believers should be living, functioning members of the Body of Christ.

I am so happy that, in the Lord's recovery, many of the new believers are able to pray for others. We are neither the clergy nor the laity, but the New Testament priests. Christ has made us such by His descension and ascension. He, as the Head of the Body, gave us as gifts to the Body. If someone were to ask us if we are gifts, each of us should declare, "Amen! Hallelujah! I'm a gift!" We were captives, sinners, and enemies of God, but through Christ's descension, we were redeemed and rescued from Satan out of sin and death. Through His ascension, He imparted Himself into us as life, so now we are living. In His ascension He made us gifts to His Body.

Many of the saints can testify that I am a gift to them. In like manner, many of the saints are gifts to me. Many times I need the small gifts to comfort me in the way that my little finger can comfort my itching ear. We should not regard the newly baptized ones as "burdens" to us. They are new gifts to the Body. When we go out as New Testament priests of the gospel to visit people, we should have the assurance that we are going to gain more gifts. These gifts are not only for Christ, but also for us.

In 1977 I encouraged all of our young people to do their best to get a proper education. One young brother among us took my fellowship and went back to school. Eventually, he graduated with a Ph.D. in linguistics and specialized in Greek. In these past few years, he has rendered a great amount of help to me in helping us to improve, to revise, our present Recovery Version. I was bearing a heavy burden to revise our version, but my knowledge of Greek is inadequate for this task. This young brother, who took my fellowship twelve years ago to go back to school, has become a great gift to me. He has been like an arm or a shoulder to me. We all can be such gifts. Thank the Lord for the gifts given by the ascended Head to His Body for its intrinsic building up.

By the Head-given Gifts— the Apostles, Prophets, Evangelists, and Shepherds and Teachers—Perfecting the Saints

The intrinsic building up of the church is by the Head-given gifts—the apostles, prophets, evangelists, and shepherds and teachers—perfecting the saints (Eph. 4:11-12). These are particular gifts such as Paul, Peter, Martin Luther, John Nelson Darby, and so forth. These Head-given gifts perfect the saints in the local churches (1 Cor. 12:28; Acts 13:1). When they are perfecting in the meetings, they are watering the members of the Body of Christ (1 Cor. 3:6b). If we come to these meetings, we will receive much watering.

The perfecting of the saints by the gifts is unto the work of the ministry—the building up of the organic Body of Christ (Eph. 4:12). This perfecting should go on and on until all the members of Christ arrive at three things: at the oneness of the faith and of the full knowledge of the Son of God, at a full-grown man, and at the measure of the stature of the fullness of Christ (Eph. 4:13). The oneness of the faith does not refer to our believing action, but to what we believe in. It is the objective faith which is the entire contents of the New Testament. The entire teaching of the New Testament is what we believe, so this New Testament teaching is our Christian faith, our Christian belief.

If we are still babyish, we may be holding on to different opinions from our background which cause us to lose the oneness of the faith (Eph. 4:14). If our background is Moslem, it may be hard for us to drop some of our Moslem philosophy. The Chinese may want to keep some thought from the teachings of Confucius. Those from a Catholic background may find it difficult to be freed of their idolatrous statues and pictures. One brother who had been newly saved went to help his mother to receive Christ. Pointing to a so-called picture of Jesus on the wall, she replied, "I have had Christ on my wall for years." This is nothing more than a Catholic superstition. However, if one is babyish, he may not be able to drop the things of his background to keep the oneness of the faith. The different opinions that Christians hold may even cause them to fight.

In order to arrive at the oneness of the faith, we all need to grow. Our different opinions and different teachings, the winds of teaching (Eph. 4:14), are like toys. As we are growing, we will drop all the toys. The younger we are, the more we like toys. As a person over eighty years of age, I have no interest in any toy. The toys that we hold onto cause us to be dissenting with one another. We have to grow to arrive at the oneness of the faith and of the full knowledge of the Son of God. We need the proper realization of the New Testament faith. We also need the proper and adequate knowledge of Christ. The full knowledge of Christ, the Son of God, will save us from the toys.

We also need to arrive at a full-grown man. We may feel that we are far away from this point, but thank the Lord that we are growing. We are traveling on the way to arrive at a full-grown man. We also are on the way to arriving at the measure of the stature of the fullness of Christ. The fullness of Christ is the Body of Christ (Eph. 1:23). We grow until we arrive at the measure of the stature of the organic Body of

Christ, which is the church. The living Body of Christ has a stature, and this stature has a measure. When we grow, the measure increases, and we are on our way to arriving at the stature of the Body of Christ.

Through All the Perfected Members of the Body of Christ

In order for the church to be built up intrinsically, the ascended Head must first give the gifts. Second, the Head-given gifts, the apostles, prophets, evangelists, shepherds and teachers, perfect the saints. Then the perfected saints build up the Body directly. Some have taken the Lord's promise in Matthew 16—"I will build My church"—to say that it is not we who build the church, but Christ. They say that we are not qualified to build up the church. This concept and teaching is absolutely wrong.

Matthew 16 is not the only chapter in the Bible. The Bible also includes Ephesians 4. Ephesians 4 reveals that the Head, Christ, builds up the church by making the saints gifts, and by giving these gifts to the church for the building up of the Body of Christ. This shows that the Head does not build up the church directly. Furthermore, the gifted persons, who are used by the Head to perfect others, do not build up the church directly either. They perfect the saints, and the saints do the direct building work. Many of us in the Lord's recovery who have been under the watering, the perfecting, for a number of years have been enabled to build up the church in our locality directly. The perfected saints are the direct builders of the church.

In Ephesians 4:14 Paul expresses his desire that the saints would be no longer babes tossed by waves and carried about by every wind of teaching. If we remain as babes, we cannot bear any responsibility. We can only burden others. Whether or not we are babes will be tested. The tests will come in the form of storms. The storms have winds and waves. Are we being tossed by waves and carried about by the winds of teaching? If we are being tossed and carried about, we are babes. If we are not tossed and carried about, we are no longer babes.

The babes are carried about by every wind of teaching "in the sleight of men, in craftiness with a view to a system of error." Actually, craftiness is sleight. The word in Greek for "sleight" signifies the cheating of dice players. This craftiness is with a view to a system of error. Both sleight and craftiness are related to man, but the system of error is related to Satan. This system is not a human system, but a satanic system. Satan has made a system of all the winds of teaching to catch the babes, to distract the younger ones away from the practical oneness of the Body and the building up of the Body.

Rather than being babes, we must be those holding to truth in love to grow up into the Head, Christ, in all things (Eph. 4:15). Holding to truth means holding to what is real. According to the entire book of Ephesians, the real things in the universe are Christ as the Head and the church as His Body. We have to hold to these two things in love that we may grow up into the Head, Christ, in all things. To grow up into Christ in all things is to build up. The growing up is the building up.

We grow up into Christ, the Head, and then something issues out from Christ, the Head. "Into Christ" is for our growth. "Out from Christ" is for our function, our usefulness. On the one hand, we are growing up into Christ. On the other hand, what we do is out from Him as the source for our function, our usefulness.

Ephesians 4:16 says, "Out from whom all the Body, joined closely together and knit together through every joint of the rich supply and through the operation in measure of each one part, causes the growth of the Body unto the building up of itself in love." The Body is joined closely together through every joint of the rich supply. These are the gifted persons such as the apostles, prophets, evangelists, shepherds and teachers. Our physical body has many joints. We need many joints in the local churches. If we do not grow up into Christ, He has no way to make us a joint. In order to become a joint, we need to pray more, seek the Lord more, read the Bible more, feed on Christ more, etc. Everything with us related to Christ and the church should be "more." We would have morning watch more. Some may have a five minute morning watch, but we would have a fifteen minute morning watch. With this kind of exercise over a period of time, we may become a joint in the Body.

In the Body, some are joints, like the apostles, prophets, evangelists, and shepherds and teachers. Others are parts who operate according to their measure. Through these two categories of members, the Body grows, and this growth is unto the building up of itself in love. If we are not a joint, we must be a part. None of us can escape from being either a joint or a part. We should not think that only the joints are useful. Every part in the Body is also useful. The thighs in our physical body are not joints, but they are great parts. We need our thighs to stand because they bear our weight. No member of the Body of Christ should despise himself. We all should praise the Lord that we are either joints or parts in the organic Body of Christ.

If you are a joint, you should supply the Body with the riches of Christ. Through your contact with the Lord, you have become a joint, so you have the riches of Christ with which you can supply the Body. If you are a part, you should operate. The Body is supplied by the joints and enjoys the operation in measure of each one part for its growth. Through the joints supplying and the parts operating, all the Body causes the growth of the Body, and the growth of the Body results in the building up of itself in love.

THE ORGANIC FUNCTION OF THE CHURCH

In the Organic Body of Christ

In the organic Body of Christ, there are organic functions (Rom. 12:4-8). Because we are in this organic Body, we should be organic. Do all of us function organically in the church life? Instead of functioning organically in the church life, we may do things mechanically. We must function either as joints of supply or as parts operating. We must have something with which to supply others, or we should operate in our measure. We must function organically for the building up of the organic Body. When the entire Body is operating, the Body causes the growth of itself, resulting in it being built up in love.

In the Local Expressions of the Organic Body of Christ by the Move of the Triune God

The organic function of the church is in the local expressions of the organic Body of Christ (1 Cor. 12:28) and by the move of the Triune God in the operations of God, through the ministries of the Lord, and with the gifts of the Spirit in His manifestations to the members of the organic Body of Christ (1 Cor. 12:4-11). While we are functioning either as supplying joints or as operating parts, the Triune God, who is within us, moves together with us. In 1 Corinthians 12:4-6, the Triune God is mentioned. There are God the Father's operations, God the Son's ministries, and God the Spirit's gifts. The gifts of the Spirit are to carry out the ministries of the Lord, and the ministries of the Lord are to accomplish the operations of God the Father. The Triune God does not move apart from us. He is waiting for us. When we move, He moves. When we speak, He speaks. If we do not speak in a meeting, God cannot speak. The Spirit exercises His gifts, the Lord carries out His ministries, and God operates while we are functioning. The organic function of the church by the move of the Triune God is for the building up of the church as the organic Body of Christ, the fullness of the all-inclusive One who fills all in all.

CHAPTER FOUR

THE INTRINSIC FELLOWSHIP
OF THE CHURCHES
FOR THEIR ORGANIC RELATIONSHIP

Scripture Reading: 1 John 1:1-4; Acts 2:42; 2 Cor. 13:14; Phil. 2:1; Jude 3; 1 Tim. 3:9; 2 Tim. 4:7; Eph. 4:14; Gal. 5:20; 1 Cor. 12:28

OUTLINE

I. The intrinsic fellowship of the churches:
   A. The flow of the divine life among and through all the members of the organic Body of Christ— 1 John 1:1-4.
   B. The unique fellowship of the apostles, which is uniquely and universally of all the members of the organic Body of Christ—Acts 2:42.
   C. The fellowship of the Spirit in the regenerated spirit of all the members of the organic Body of Christ—2 Cor. 13:14; Phil. 2:1.
   D. The fellowship based on the unique belief (the faith) of all the members of the organic Body of Christ according to the teaching of the apostles— the unique teaching of the New Testament— Jude 0, 1 Tim. 3:9; 2 Tim. 4:7; Acts 2:42.
   E. Any special fellowship based on any wind of teaching being one of the three factors (a special fellowship, a special name, and a special ground) of a sect—Eph. 4:14; Gal. 5:20.
II. The organic relationship of the churches:
   A. The unique relationship of the unique church (the universal church composed of all the local churches)—1 Cor. 12:28.

B. Based on the unique and universal fellowship among all the members of the organic Body of Christ—cf. Phil. 2:1.

C. Practiced uniquely and universally among all the local churches as the unique, organic Body of Christ—the unique church in the universe.

D. No relationship limited in a local autonomy, and no federated relationship, but a unique relationship among all the local churches in the unique and universal, organic Body of Christ.

THE INTRINSIC FELLOWSHIP OF THE CHURCHES FOR THEIR ORGANIC RELATIONSHIP

In the last three chapters, we have seen three intrinsic matters related to the church: the church's intrinsic essence, intrinsic growth, and intrinsic building up. The fourth intrinsic matter is the intrinsic fellowship of the churches for their organic relationship. The Greek word for fellowship is *koinonia,* meaning joint participation, common participation. This is a very sweet term, but it is difficult to get the proper, accurate, adequate, and equivalent term in the English language. The problem is that the proper meaning of the term *fellowship,* along with many other crucial terms in the Bible, has been spoiled by the traditional or religious interpretation in Christianity. To some, fellowship is "socializing." Many people go to the denominational services for this reason. They have some form of worship, but their main interest is in socializing with one another. We must drop such a degraded concept. Our understanding of "fellowship" should be according to the pure Word of God.

THE INTRINSIC FELLOWSHIP OF THE CHURCHES

The Flow of the Divine Life among and through All the Members of the Organic Body of Christ

The intrinsic fellowship of the churches is the flow of the divine life among and through all the members of the organic Body of Christ (1 John 1:1-4). First John 1:1-2 says, "That which was from the beginning, which we have heard, which we have seen with our eyes, which we beheld, and our hands handled concerning the Word of life; and the life was manifested, and we have seen and testify and report to you the eternal life, which was with the Father and was manifested to us." The "Word" mentioned here is unique, not common. John also uses this term in his Gospel. John 1:1 says, "In the beginning was the Word, and the Word was with God, and the Word was God." The unique Word was in the beginning. In eternity past, there was the Word. The Word which was in the beginning was with God and was God. The Word in 1 John 1 is the same Word mentioned in John 1. In John's Gospel, he introduced us to this Word. In his Epistle, he refers us back to this same Word, who is God Himself.

This Word is the Word of life. God is life, the Word which is God is life to us, and this life was manifested. This life is the Lord Jesus Christ. When He was manifested in His flesh, He was manifested as life. If we prayerfully consider the record in the four Gospels with all the stories recorded concerning Jesus, we can see that in His human living, life was always manifested. The Lord Jesus was a person who manifested life. The disciples, including John, saw that life. Therefore, John could testify and report to us the eternal life which was with the Father.

In the Gospel of John, the Word was God, and the Word became flesh and tabernacled among the disciples (1:14). John is reporting to us that which he saw and heard. He had heard, seen and even handled the Word of life, which is the eternal life. Now he is testifying and reporting to us the eternal life. Then John goes on to say that he reported what he had seen and heard, not that we might have "life" but that we might have "fellowship." First John 1:3 says, "That which we have seen and heard we report also to you, that you also may have fellowship with us, and indeed the fellowship which is ours is with the Father and with His Son Jesus Christ." At this point John uses another word to replace the word "life." They saw and heard life, and they reported life, but it was for a strong purpose. John was saying, "We report to you life with the strong purpose that you may have fellowship with us." This is the "fellowship which is ours." "Ours" refers to the apostles. The fellowship which is ours, the apostles' fellowship, is with the Father and with His Son Jesus Christ. They report the Son as life to us that we may share this fellowship with them. Then in 1 John 1:4, John says, "These things we write that our joy may be made full." The apostles would be happy to see that the believers would have what they have. What they have is fellowship with the Father and the Son. If the believers participate in this fellowship, they will be happy.

There are three major points we need to see when we study the significance of fellowship in the first four verses of 1 John 1. First, fellowship is something of the divine life.

Second, this fellowship is the apostles' fellowship. Third, the apostles expected to see that the believers would share in this fellowship. When we say that this fellowship is something of life, we mean that it is the flow of the divine life. It is the issue of the eternal life and is actually the flow of the eternal life within all the believers who have received and possess the divine life.

The divine life flows. At the conclusion of the Bible, the last chapter of Revelation gives us quite a meaningful picture. There is the throne of God and of the Lamb (Rev. 22:1). Out of this throne proceeds a current, a flow, which is the flow of the water of life, and this flow is a river. When a flow becomes a river, it is a very strong flow. The river in Revelation is the river of water of life (Rev. 22:1).

The last two chapters of Revelation present a picture of the New Jerusalem, a foursquare city which is a high mountain, twelve thousand stadia high (Rev. 21:16-17). There are three gates on each of the four sides of the city (Rev. 21:12-13). At the top of the mountain is the throne of God and of the Lamb. A river flows out from the throne and reaches every part of the city because it spirals down the mountain from the throne and passes by all twelve gates of the city. There is only one river, flowing in the one street (22:1) and watering every part of the city. Since the river is a spiral, it will pass through everywhere in the holy city, no matter where you are in it. This is a physical picture showing us the invisible things of the Spirit.

Today God is on the throne. Surely, He is on the throne in the heavens, but if the throne were just in the heavens, it would be too far for us to reach. Hebrews 4:16 charges us to "come forward with boldness to the throne of grace." If the throne of grace were so far away, we could not reach it during our morning watch with the Lord. When we come to the Lord in the morning, however, we can touch Him on the throne of grace right away. This is because the throne is not only in the heavens but also in our spirit (see note 1 on Hebrews 4:16, Recovery Version). A river flows out of the throne. Within us there is a river that not only flows but also spirals to reach every part of our being. According to the picture in Revelation, the river flows to reach all twelve gates of the entire city. This

river of water of life is the fellowship of the divine life which
John speaks of in his first Epistle.

It may help us to understand this fellowship, this flow
of the divine life, if we consider the circulation of blood in
our human body. There is only one circulation of blood in our
body, and it reaches every member of our body. No member of
our physical body is independently autonomous of the other
members. All the members of the body participate in the one
blood circulation. There are many members, but only one flow
of blood. The intrinsic element of the human body is its blood.
This circulation of blood in our human body is a picture of the
intrinsic fellowship in the Body of Christ.

Whatever the church is, is intrinsic. It cannot be divided.
The essence of the church is intrinsic, its growth is intrinsic,
and its building up is intrinsic. Furthermore, the fellowship of
the churches is also intrinsic, just as the blood circulation
within our body is intrinsic. The local churches as the unique,
organic Body of Christ, cannot be separately autonomous
since they participate in the one intrinsic fellowship, the one
flow of the divine life.

If our physical body were divided into autonomies, we would
be good for nothing but a funeral. The members of our physical
body are not autonomous, nor are they federated together. The
United States of America may be considered as an organized
federation of fifty states. Our government is a federal government. The fifty states are not divided but federated together as
one nation. The church, however, is neither autonomous nor
federated because the church is not organized like a country.
The church is the universal Body of Christ, an organism.

Our physical body is a picture of the Body of Christ (Rom.
12:4-5). Our body has only one head, yet there are many members under this one head. All the members have only one head,
and according to the blood circulation with the nerves, every
member is connected to the head directly. The blood circulation, however, does not reach the members directly. It must
flow through other members. The picture we need to see is
that the blood circulation in our body is intrinsically one. In
like manner, the fellowship, the flow of life in the Body of
Christ, is intrinsically and uniquely one. The flow of blood in

our physical body is a good illustration of the fellowship, the flow of the divine life.

When we believed in the Lord Jesus, we were brought into this fellowship. When we called on the name of the Lord, we may say that the Spirit came into us, that God came into us, or that the divine life came into us. When we believed in the Lord Jesus, we received Him into us, and He is the Spirit (2 Cor. 3:17). The Spirit is the consummation of the Triune God, and the Triune God is the divine life. The One who is now in us is the divine life, which is the Triune God, who is the Spirit and who is Jesus Christ. The divine, eternal life is a person, Jesus Christ. This One is the life-giving Spirit (1 Cor. 15:45b), and this life-giving Spirit is the consummation of the Triune God. The consummation of the Triune God is within us as the divine life, and this divine life is flowing within us all the time. He is flowing within you, within me, and within all the members of His great, universal Body. Within His universal Body is one flow, the flow of the divine life, the current of the water of life. The water is the divine life, and the divine life is the Triune God. The Triune God flows!

The first stanza of *Hymns,* #12 says:

> O God, Thou art the source of life,
> Divine, and rich and free!
> As living water flowing out
> Unto eternity!

God is a flowing river who flows in all His chosen and redeemed believers. This flow is the fellowship of the divine life. According to 2 Corinthians 13:14, this is the fellowship within the Triune God. This verse says, "The grace of the Lord Jesus Christ, and the love of God, and the fellowship of the Holy Spirit be with you all." The Father is the source as love. Out of this love, grace comes forth through the Son. This grace through the Son reaches us as the fellowship of the Spirit, who is the consummation of the Triune God. The love of God in the grace of Christ becomes the fellowship, the flow, of the Holy Spirit. This fellowship has been neglected and even ignored by many Christians. Very few Christians know this flow. If you know this flow, you are greatly blessed.

The Unique Fellowship of the Apostles, Which Is Uniquely and Universally of All the Members of the Organic Body of Christ

The intrinsic fellowship of the churches is the unique fellowship of the apostles, which is uniquely and universally of all the members of the organic Body of Christ (Acts 2:42). The flow was first the fellowship of the divine life of the divine Trinity. Then this fellowship was passed on to the apostles, who were among the first group of believers on earth. Therefore, this flow became the fellowship of the apostles. All of the early apostles were in the flow of the divine life. Furthermore, in those early days, all the believers continued steadfastly in the teaching and the fellowship of the apostles. There was only one teaching and one fellowship. The apostles did a wonderful work to impart the divine life into people and bring them into the flow of this divine life. This flow, this fellowship, became the new believers' fellowship. Their fellowship was the fellowship of the apostles, and the fellowship of the apostles is the fellowship of the Triune God.

The Three of the Godhead are fellowshipping among Themselves. This fellowship among the Three of the Triune God is with the apostles, and it is also with us. We must realize that today in the universe, there is a flow which is just God Himself as the water of life flowing out of the Triune God through the apostles and into us. He not only flows into us, but also through us into new believers. When we preach the gospel and the ones to whom we preach receive the Lord Jesus, we are giving them an "injection" of the water of life. When they receive the water of life, they are brought into this wonderful fellowship.

We may not fully understand this fellowship, yet it is a wonderful fact. Whenever we meet a genuine believer, no matter what nationality or race he may be, something "jumps" within us. This experience may be compared to what happened when Mary, the mother of Jesus, went to see Elizabeth, the mother of John the Baptist. When Elizabeth heard Mary's greeting, the baby leaped in her womb (Luke 1:41). Something within her was leaping. John the Baptist exulted (v. 44) upon meeting the

Savior, while both of them were still in their mothers' wombs. We may say that there was a fellowship between John the Baptist and Jesus Christ even before they were born. Today we are the "mothers" who have the Lord Jesus within us. When we Christians meet one another, something within us "jumps." We have to go along with the "jumping" within us. That inward "jumping" is the intrinsic fellowship.

This intrinsic, unique fellowship is among all the members of the Body of Christ to make them one, regardless of their outward differences in race or culture. When I was a youth, the Chinese people hated the Japanese because they had invaded China. I was brought up in that atmosphere, but the Lord saved me, and in 1933 I was called by the Lord to quit my job and serve Him full-time. The same day that I dropped my job, I received an invitation from Manchuria, inviting me to speak. While I was speaking there, some Japanese believers came to me, told me that they were Christians, and invited me to come to their place to share with them. I went to their place and met with them according to their custom. Even though I had grown up in an atmosphere in which there was much hatred for the Japanese people, something was "jumping" within me as I met with them because they were my Christian brothers. I loved them, and I was so happy to meet with them. My love for them was something in the flow of the divine life, the fellowship, within me.

If we follow the intrinsic fellowship, there will be no problems between us. When we are centered on the outward things, trouble comes. In some places in the United States, the white people and the black people would not meet together to worship the Lord. This is because of their centering on outward things rather than on the intrinsic fellowship. Problems among the saints are also due to focusing on something outward rather than on the intrinsic fellowship of life.

Christians love one another until they focus on outward things such as what group they meet with or what doctrines they agree on. One Christian may believe in pre-tribulation rapture, while another believes in post-tribulation rapture. They may argue and fight over their doctrinal disagreements. As long as we are centered on doctrines, there will be division.

There are many doctrines, but there is only one intrinsic fellowship. If we only care for the intrinsic fellowship, the flow of the divine life, which is like the blood circulation in our body, we will be fine. We must limit ourselves to the flow, the fellowship of the divine life. We should live in and care for this intrinsic fellowship, which is of the Triune God, of the apostles, and of all the believers.

The Fellowship of the Spirit
in the Regenerated Spirit of All the Members
of the Organic Body of Christ

The intrinsic fellowship of the churches is the fellowship of the Spirit in the regenerated spirit of all the members of the organic Body of Christ (2 Cor. 13:14; Phil. 2:1). Second Corinthians 13:14 refers to the "fellowship of the Holy Spirit," and Philippians 2:1 mentions "fellowship of spirit," indicating the human spirit. Therefore, the intrinsic fellowship is of the divine Spirit residing in our human spirit.

We believers come from many different backgrounds and cultures. Regardless of our differences outwardly, however, we all have the same intrinsic fellowship. Japanese, Korean, black, and white all become one in this fellowship. If we do not follow the outward things, but follow only our spirit with the Spirit, we are in the flow. In the Lord's recovery, we practice this universal oneness in the flow of the divine life. Many have testified that our meetings are a wonder because all the races are meeting together as one. We can meet as one because we care only for the intrinsic fellowship.

The Fellowship Based on
the Unique Belief (the Faith)
of All the Members of the Organic Body of Christ
according to the Teaching of the Apostles—
the Unique Teaching of the New Testament

The fellowship is based on the unique belief (the faith) of all the members of the organic Body of Christ according to the teaching of the apostles—the unique teaching of the New Testament (Jude 3; 1 Tim. 3:9; 2 Tim. 4:7; Acts 2:42). We all have to know our faith, the objective faith. This faith is our

Christian belief, the things in which we believe, not our believing act. All the members of the organic Body of Christ have a fellowship which is based on the faith, the unique belief. Whatever we believe is according to the teaching of the apostles, the unique teaching of the New Testament.

Any Special Fellowship Based on Any Wind of Teaching Being One of the Three Factors (a Special Fellowship, a Special Name, and a Special Ground) of a Sect

The fellowship among believers must not be based on any wind of teaching (Eph. 4:14). If our fellowship is based upon different teachings that are winds, these teachings will be one of the three factors of a sect: a special fellowship, a special name, or a special ground. Any of the three will cause us to become a sect or division (Gal. 5:20). Therefore, we must avoid any special fellowship which is based on any wind of teaching.

THE ORGANIC RELATIONSHIP OF THE CHURCHES

The Unique Relationship of the Unique Church (the Universal Church Composed of All the Local Churches)

The organic relationship of the churches is the unique relationship of the unique church—the universal church composed of all the local churches (1 Cor. 12:28). Today in the Lord's recovery, there are about eleven hundred fifty churches throughout the earth. There are many local churches, but there is only one unique, universal, and intrinsic fellowship which is for the organic relationship of the churches.

No Relationship Limited in a Local Autonomy, and No Federated Relationship, but a Unique Relationship among All the Local Churches in the Unique and Universal, Organic Body of Christ

The elders of each of the local churches should consider what kind of relationship they have with the other churches. Is their relationship limited to the brothers in their locality, or are they in fellowship with all the churches in the Lord's recovery? The leading brothers in a certain locality may have "private talks" with one another. When another leading brother from another locality comes to join them, they may then stop their talk. Before the other leading brother joined them, they talked freely. When he arrived, they stopped their talk. This leading brother was excluded from their private relationship. Two churches may be very close to one another geographically, and yet their relationship is separate. These two churches may not want to let each other know about their affairs. It is hard to see two elders from two different churches talking freely. Do not misunderstand what I am trying to say here. I am not for the federation of the churches, nor am I for their autonomy. I am only for the unique and universal fellowship which is for the organic relationship among all the churches. The relationship of every church should be the unique, universal fellowship of the divine life. In this fellowship, the churches should not have anything private, except certain cases of individuals, involving confidential and personal matters.

Some may say, "Don't the churches keep their accounts separately?" Two leading brothers may be talking about their financial situation locally, but when a leading brother from another locality joins them, they may change the subject. They want to keep their account private. But our finances are not something that we need to keep secret. There is nothing wrong with a poor local church, which is short of money, fellowshipping with some other churches to let these churches know their need. Otherwise, how can one church discover the needs of another? There may be a church which is quite rich, having a large surplus of funds. If this church does not have the liberty to ask concerning another church's needs, how will it be able to help? The surplus of a local church is not just their surplus. It is the surplus of the Body. It is altogether right for a rich church to tell the poor churches that they have a surplus. It is also right for the poor churches to tell the rich ones about their needs. One church may have material surplus, whereas three other churches may be in desperate need. If our relationship is only limited to our locality, the Body of Christ suffers greatly.

What I am talking about is not the way of federation. We do not want to have a federation. The way we should take is the way based upon the unique and universal fellowship of the churches. Some brothers overseeing a needy church in a certain locality may be too proud to tell the other churches that they are in need. This is wrong. This kind of pride causes separation. There is absolutely nothing wrong with this needy church taking the opportunity to fellowship with another local church who has more money. The church who has the surplus should consider the need of the needy church as their need. The Bible frequently charges us to take care of those in need. If we care for individuals in this way, should we not care for the churches in the same way? The churches are not divided or separated, regardless of how far they are from one another geographically. The churches are one. How good it is that the churches can go on together in oneness!

The churches should not keep matters related to their going on with the Lord private, but as we have mentioned, there are individual cases within a local church that must be kept private. If someone is in immorality or some sinful situation, this must be a private matter within that local church. Such matters should be kept secret. To expose the personal matters of others that are shared with us in confidence is unlawful. Medical doctors are not allowed to expose the defects of their patients. Pastors are not allowed to publicly expose the moral failures of their church members. This is unlawful. A local church is not for condemning people. It is for rescuing, recovering, and loving people. The church has not been commissioned to condemn people or to "arrest" people like a police station. A local church should be a loving organ that loves the sinners, the backsliders, and the fallen ones. Its function is not to condemn but to rescue.

Galatians 6:1 says that if one among us is overtaken by some sin, we should exercise a spirit of meekness to recover him. A part of the word *recover* is the word *cover*. When we are attempting to recover someone, we must cover him. To cover is to protect. We should protect a sinful one. This does not mean, however, that we tolerate the sin. We cannot tolerate the sin, but we must take care of the sinful matter privately with a view to rescuing the sinning one. There is no need for other churches to know about this kind of situation.

For the need and going on of the churches, however, there is the need of much fellowship. All the local churches are one church. There is an organic relationship among all the churches. Their relationship is not organizational. The relationship of the churches must be organic according to the divine life and based upon the organic fellowship of the divine life. If we keep this view, we will be saved from many problems.

When the first group of apostles was on the earth, the churches were organically one. After a time, however, the churches began to degrade and became divided. In the beginning of the fourth century, in 325 A.D., Constantine called a council at Nicea. He presided over that council to force all the principal teachers of that day to be one. Eventually, the issue of this kind of endeavor was the formation of the Catholic Church. Actually, there is nothing wrong with being "catholic" in the proper sense. To be catholic is to be universal or all-inclusive. In the proper sense, all the churches should be "catholic"; they should be universally one. The word "catholic," however, has been spoiled. The Catholic Church has created a great hierarchy. This hierarchy came out of the erroneous teaching of Ignatius that an overseer, a bishop, is higher than an elder. From this erroneous teaching came the hierarchy of bishops, archbishops, cardinals, and the pope in the Catholic Church. This teaching is also the source of the episcopal system of ecclesiastical government. Such hierarchy annuls the headship of Christ. We should hate such a hierarchical practice.

When the Brethren were raised up, they strongly attacked the hierarchical practice of Catholicism. Eventually, however, the Brethren became divided over their doctrinal teachings. John Nelson Darby was accused of attempting to unify the churches in the way of federation. One teacher, G. H. Lang, in reacting against Darby, taught that every local assembly should be autonomous. This teaching of autonomy ruined the Brethren, causing division after division.

In relation to the church, the practice of autonomy is wrong, and the practice of federation is also wrong. The church is neither federated nor autonomous. We should only care to practice the Body life of the church as the organism of the Triune God. In the Lord's recovery, we do not practice autonomy or federation. We only have a practice based upon the unique and universal fellowship in the Body of Christ. The church in one locality should not have the attitude that they have nothing to do with the church in another locality. We have to admit that such an intrinsic realization of the separate, autonomous relationship of the churches has been creeping into and, even to some extent, has been existing in the recovery. This realization is intrinsically wrong. The churches should not practice having a separate, autonomous relationship among one another. It is also wrong for the churches to practice a federated relationship. We should practice the unique relationship based upon the unique, universal, fellowship of the Body of Christ.

The organic relationship of the churches is based on the unique and universal fellowship among all the members of the organic Body of Christ (cf. Phil. 2:1). This organic relationship is practiced uniquely and universally among all the local churches as the unique, organic Body of Christ—the unique church in the universe. The churches should have no relationship limited in a local autonomy, and no federated relationship, but a unique relationship among all the local churches in the unique and universal, organic Body of Christ.

CHAPTER FIVE

THE INTRINSIC FACTOR
OF THE WINDS OF TEACHING
FOR THEIR PURPOSE

Scripture Reading: Matt. 13:19; 1 Tim. 1:3-4; 6:3; Eph. 4:14;
2 Tim. 2:18; Acts 8:3; 1 Cor. 1:10-11; Phil. 1:15-18; 3:2

OUTLINE

I. The intrinsic factor of the winds of teaching:
   A. The winds of teaching:
      1. The winds:
         a. The devilish blowings of the evil one—
            Matt. 13:19.
         b. Bringing storms into the church.
      2. The blowing teachings:
         a. Different from the New Testament teaching concerning the economy of God for the building up of the unique and organic Body of Christ—1 Tim. 1:3-4; 6:3.
         b. Like the teachings of Judaism, Gnosticism, etc., in the ancient times, and like the teaching of the absolute autonomy of a local church, of no delegated authority, of democracy instead of theocracy, of no spiritual father, etc., in the present time.
   B. The intrinsic factor of such blowing teachings:
      1. The sleight of men—man's subtle ways of cheating.
      2. That is, the craftiness of men with a view to a system of error—man's plotted deception to induce people into the satanic system of error—Eph. 4:14.

II. The purpose of the winds of teaching:
  A. The evil purpose of the enemy Satan versus the eternal economy of God.
  B. To overthrow the faith of some believers—2 Tim. 2:18.
  C. To devastate the church life—Acts 8:3.
  D. To frustrate the building up of the organic Body of Christ.
  E. To tear down the building up of the organic Body of Christ.
  F. To divide the members of the organic Body of Christ—causing endless divisions (sects) in hatred and jealousy, instead of keeping the unique oneness of the Body of Christ in love and kindness—1 Cor. 1:10-11.

THE INTRINSIC FACTOR OF THE WINDS OF TEACHING FOR THEIR PURPOSE

Prayer: Lord, how we thank You that You have brought us through the past four meetings. Our trust is still in You. We do not have any trust in ourselves. Lord, our trust is in Your blessing. Without Your blessing, we cannot do anything. Lord, cover us, cleanse us, and forgive us of all our sinfulness. Be with us. Grant us Your rich anointing with Your holy ointment. We need this. We need Your presence. We need Your up-to-date speaking. We need Your speaking in our speaking. Lord, vindicate Your recovery. We want to be one with You, in one spirit with You. Lord, defeat the enemy and gain the victory for Your kingdom and for Your spreading. Gain the victory in the preaching of the gospel, in the home meetings, in the perfecting of the saints, and in the prophesying for the organic building up of Your Body. Lord, while we are fighting for Your kingdom, we could never forget our enemy who is Your enemy. We accuse him before Your throne of authority. Lord, we ask You to defeat him and shame him to the uttermost. May all the glory be Yours, and may all the blessings be upon us. Thank You. Amen.

In the previous chapters, we have covered four intrinsic matters of the church. In this chapter we come to another intrinsic matter which is negative—the intrinsic factor of the winds of teaching for their purpose. The four previous chapters on the positive intrinsic matters of the church may be considered as fellowship related to the "day." The fellowship in this chapter may be considered as something related to the "night." According to God's creation, there is both day and night; there is morning and evening. We need the day and we also need the night. During the night, there are the moon and the stars. The moon typifies the church (S. S. 6:10), and the stars typify the saints (Dan. 12:3; Matt. 5:14; Phil. 2:15). The moon and the stars shine during the night. For our shining, we need the night. Of course, we also need the day, in which Christ shines as the sun (Mal. 4:2; Luke 1:78-79). Christ shines in the day, but He is reflected in the night by the moon, the church, and He shines in the night through the stars, the saints. In the night the church and the saints are shining. In this chapter we will fellowship about something in the "night," but this fellowship will be under the shining light of the church and of the saints, the moon and the stars.

THE INTRINSIC FACTOR OF THE WINDS OF TEACHING

Now that we have seen the intrinsic essence, intrinsic growth, intrinsic building up, and intrinsic fellowship of the church, we need to see the intrinsic factor of the winds of teaching for their purpose. An intrinsic factor is a hidden factor. It is a factor that is not apparent. To see this intrinsic factor, we need a proper and sharp understanding that can penetrate into the whole situation. Every wind of teaching apparently is very good. If it were not good in appearance, nobody would accept it. However, within the winds of teaching, intrinsically, is something different that is not good.

Ephesians 4:14 says, "That we may be no longer babes tossed by waves and carried about by every wind of teaching in the sleight of men, in craftiness with a view to a system of error." "In the sleight of men" is in apposition to "in craftiness," which is "with a view to a system of error." The sleight in this verse is of men, and the system of error is of Satan. Man has the sleight, the craftiness, but man is not able to have a system in this universe. Satan is the one who is able to have a system of error. Man's sleight, man's craftiness, is related to the satanic system of error.

Ephesians 4:14 may be considered as the conclusion of the history of Christianity. Christianity is full of the sleight, the craftiness, of men. The word for "sleight" in Greek signifies the cheating of dice players. A crafty gambler knows how to play dice in order to cheat his opponent. The sleight of men is a cheating method. This method of cheating is crafty, so it becomes craftiness. The sleight of men implies the cheating and deception of men. The history of Christianity shows us that there can be cheating and deception in a so-called Christian teaching.

The Winds of Teaching

We need to see what the winds of teaching are. These winds are the devilish blowings of the evil one. In Matthew

13:19, the Lord said, "When anyone hears the word of the kingdom and does not understand, the evil one comes and snatches away that which has been sown in his heart." The evil one is Satan (1 John 5:19). Satan, the evil one, is also the one who sowed the tares, the false believers, amidst the true ones (Matt. 13:25, 38-39). The tares resemble the wheat, and it is impossible to discern the difference between them until the fruit is produced at the time of their maturity. The fruit of the wheat is golden yellow, but the fruit of the tares is black. The sowing of the tares, who are the sons of the evil one (Matt. 13:38), was the work of Satan, the evil one. His evil purpose in doing this was to corrupt God's children, who are the wheat.

The devilish blowings of the evil one bring storms into the church. I have been in the church life for about sixty years, and I have seen many such storms. I was with Brother Nee in the work for eighteen years, and during that period of time there were three or four storms, which was about one storm every five years. I came out of mainland China to Taiwan in 1949 and eventually I came to the United States in 1962. In these past forty years, we have had a storm about every twelve years. A storm is created by winds and waves. Ephesians 4:14 talks about being tossed by waves and carried about by every wind of teaching. When the wind comes, the waves follow. The wind plus the waves equals a storm. From my years of experience, I realize that we do not need to feel threatened by a storm. No storm comes and stays forever. The storm comes, and the storm goes.

The teachings that become winds are the "blowing teachings." These teachings are different from the New Testament teaching concerning the economy of God for the building up of the unique and organic Body of Christ (1 Tim. 1:3-4; 6:3). First Timothy 1:3-4 says, "Even as I urged you, when I was going into Macedonia, to remain in Ephesus in order that you might charge certain ones not to teach differently, nor to occupy themselves with myths and unending genealogies, which give occasion for questionings rather than God's dispensation which is in faith." Ephesus was the place where Paul stayed purposely for three years. In Acts 20 Paul said that within those three years, he taught publicly and from house to house, did not cease admonishing each one with tears, and did not shrink from declaring to the saints all the counsel of God (vv. 20, 31, 27). The counsel of God, no doubt, refers to the economy of God, the eternal plan of God. Paul taught God's economy night and day, publicly in the meetings and personally from house to house. Paul did not shrink from telling the saints in Ephesus anything that was profitable to them, which no doubt, included the things in their daily life. Paul had done so much for the church in Ephesus, but years later he was still greatly concerned about the church there. When he was going into Macedonia, he charged Timothy to remain in Ephesus in order that Timothy might charge certain ones not to teach differently. Not many, but certain ones were teaching differently. This means that even at Paul's time there were some who were teaching things different from Paul's teaching.

"God's dispensation" in 1 Timothy 1:4 is "God's economy." The word *economy* is the anglicized form of the Greek word *oikonomia*. *Oikonomia* is composed of two Greek words: *oikos* meaning house and *nomos* meaning law. Therefore, *oikonomia* is the law of the house, the regulation of the family, or the household administration. God has a great, universal house, and God has His law, His regulation, His administration concerning His house. This household administration is God's economy. God's economy, which is in faith, carries out the dispensing of God Himself. God in His divine Trinity—the Father, the Son, and the Spirit—is for the dispensing of Himself into His believers. God's economy is God's household administration for dispensing Himself into His chosen people. This is the central lane of the New Testament teaching.

The New Testament teaches how the Triune God was incarnated to be a man. This God-man lived a holy life, a righteous life, a bright life, a life of light. He lived such a life for thirty-three and a half years. After He finished such a testimony in His human living, He died on the cross an all-inclusive death. His death solved all the problems in the universe related to God and us. After coming out of death, He entered into another stage, the stage of resurrection. In resurrection He was begotten to be God's firstborn Son, the Firstborn among many brothers (Acts 13:33; Rom. 8:29). In resurrection He also became a life-giving Spirit (1 Cor. 15:45b), imparting Himself into us, His believers, to be our life, making us the sons of God. Before His resurrection, God had only one Son, His only begotten Son. But in resurrection God gained many sons who are the many brothers of the firstborn Son, Christ.

As we have seen in chapter three, these sons were brought by the Son to the Father, and offered to the Father as a corporate present (Psa. 68:18; Eph. 4:8). Then God the Father in His economy returned this present to the Son as gifts. Then the Son gave these gifts to His Body for its building up (Eph. 4:11-12). It is wonderful that all of us believers are gifts to function in the Body of Christ for the building up of the Body of Christ. We are gifts to the Body of Christ and are working for the Body of Christ that the Body of Christ may grow, may increase, may be built up, to arrive at the measure of the stature of the fullness of Christ. When we arrive at this state, the bride will be prepared, and the Bridegroom, Christ, will come to have His wedding. I am hoping and expecting to be a part of that bride, to be ready for the marriage of the Lamb, the universal Bridegroom (Rev. 19:7-9). As the gifts who were given by the Son from the Father to the churches, we are working and preparing for this coming wedding.

The entire twenty-seven books of the New Testament stress one thing: God's New Testament economy, the contents of which is the Triune God passing through the processes of incarnation, human living, an all-inclusive death, and resurrection to become the life giving Spirit and to produce the Body of Christ which is to be expressed in many localities as the local churches. This is God's economy, and we should not teach anything other than this. We need to teach God's economy in an intrinsic way. Then we will speak the same thing that the New Testament speaks. To teach anything other than God's economy is to teach something different from what the New Testament teaches. We need to keep ourselves in the central lane of God's New Testament economy. Then we will not be involved in or influenced by the different teachings, the blowing teachings.

The blowing teachings are like the teachings of Judaism, Gnosticism, etc., in the ancient times and like the teaching of the absolute autonomy of a local church, of no delegated authority, of democracy instead of theocracy, of no spiritual father, etc., in the present time. The Judaizers in Paul's day propagated Judaism, and they also preached the gospel. Philippians 1:15-18 records that these ones preached the gospel in rivalry with and in jealousy of Paul. In 3:2 Paul called them the unclean dogs, the evil workers, and the contemptible concision. "Concision," meaning mutilation, is a term of contempt for circumcision. Henry Alford points out in his commentary on Philippians that the dogs, evil workers, and concision referred to in Philippians 3 are those who preached the gospel in rivalry with Paul referred to in chapter one. These ones preached the gospel, but actually they were evil workers. The teaching of these Judaizers was a wind that would "blow away" some of the saints from the central lane of Christ and the church. Also at Paul's time there were the Gnostics, who preached their form of Greek wisdom. They also taught differently from Paul's teaching focused on God's New Testament economy in order to frustrate the building up of the organic Body of Christ.

Today there are also teachings that are winds to carry us away from God's central purpose. We have pointed out that the teaching concerning the absolute autonomy of a local church has been creeping into the Lord's recovery. A book by G. H. Lang entitled *The Churches of God* was promoted by some brothers. In this book Lang talks about the autonomy of the local church. The teaching of autonomy ruined the Brethren assemblies. Within a short period of time, the Brethren became divided into many divisions. In one locality the Brethren would have five separate, autonomous assemblies. I know of one Brethren assembly which was split over whether to use a piano or an organ in their meetings. Because of this disagreement, they divided into two assemblies. One assembly used the piano, and the other assembly used the organ.

In 1933 Brother Nee was invited to visit the Brethren in

England. Then he went to the United States and Canada to visit the Brethren there. When he returned from his trip, he reported to us how the Brethren assemblies were divided. He told us that their situation was one of confusion. Even in one city there could be many Brethren assemblies. This caused Brother Nee to study the Bible again to find out the boundary of a local assembly, a local church. In 1934 he published a book entitled *The Assembly Life*. In that book of four chapters, he told us that the boundary and the jurisdiction of a local assembly, a local church, is the boundary of the city in which it is. Three years later, in 1937, Brother Nee saw and shared more concerning the ground of the church. This truth is in *The Normal Christian Church Life*. In this book he pointed out that because the boundary of a local church is the boundary of the city in which the church is, the ground on which a local church can be built up, based on the unique oneness of the Body of Christ, is also the city in which the church is. To teach that the local churches are absolutely autonomous is to divide the Body of Christ.

Another wind of teaching in the present day is the teaching of no delegated authority. Some say that there is no authority appointed by God to represent God on this earth. But the Bible tells us clearly that the husband is the head of the wife (Eph. 5:23) and that the head of the woman is the man (1 Cor. 11:3). The Bible also indicates clearly that the parents are the delegated authority of God over their children (Eph. 6:1-3; Col. 3:20). Romans 13 tells us that human governments are God's delegated authorities to rule over this earth.

Consider what marriage life would be like if the husband were not the head. What if there were no government in a city or a country? There would be a situation of anarchy and lawlessness. If there were no police in a major city, that city would be full of disorder, chaos, and uncontrolled crime. The husband as the head of the wife is the delegated authority of God for the family; the parents are the delegated authorities for their children; and the governments are delegated authorities which God uses to rule this earth. These governmental authorities work so that we can minister Christ to one another and preach the gospel in a peaceful, orderly, lawful environment. The teaching of no delegated authority is not found in the Bible.

There is also delegated authority in the Body of Christ. The New Testament shows us clearly that in the local church there must be a government with elders appointed by apostles (Acts 14:23; Titus 1:5). The Bible tells us that the elders are the leading ones (Rom. 12:8). If we would maintain a good order in the house of God, we must have the leading ones, and according to Hebrews 13:17, all the saints should obey them and submit to them. This is necessary for the building up of the church.

The apostles appoint elders in the churches they raise up (Acts 14:23), and the elders still have to receive the instructions and leading from the apostles (1 Tim. 3:14-15; Titus 1:5-9; Acts 20:17-18a, 28-32, 35), although the responsibility for the care and the leading of the church is entrusted to the elders. Not only do the apostles have the duty and authority to appoint elders, they also have the duty and authority to remove them. Paul said to Timothy, "Against an elder do not receive an accusation, except on the word of two or three witnesses. Those who sin reprove before all that the rest also may be in fear" (1 Tim. 5:19-20). This indicates that after an apostle has chosen and appointed men to be elders, he still has the authority to deal with them. This brief fellowship should help us to see that the teaching of no delegated authority is a wind of teaching to frustrate and tear down the organic building up of the Body of Christ.

Another wind of teaching today is the teaching of democracy instead of theocracy. God's administration is neither by autocracy nor by democracy but by theocracy. Theocracy is government by God with God's authority. The nation of Israel in the Old Testament was a theocracy. God exercised His administration through the priests by means of the Urim and the Thummim on the breastplate (Exo. 28:30; Lev. 8:8; Num. 27:21; Deut. 33:8; 1 Sam. 28:6; Ezra 2:63; Neh. 7:65). This was God's government in typology. In the New Testament, in the church, there should also be theocracy. Today the Urim and the Thummim in reality are within us. The reality of the Urim and the Thummim is the Triune God as Christ, who is the life-giving Spirit in us. Today we manage the churches according to the leading of the Spirit within us. This is our Urim and Thummim today.

It is all right for the people of the world to want democracy. Humanly speaking, democracy is a wonderful form of government. However, it is a shame to have democracy in the church. This means that anyone can speak anything they please. A local church that practices democracy is like the church in Laodicea (Rev. 3:14). "Laodicea" in Greek means the opinion of the people. The church in Laodicea typifies the church in degradation. The "germs" of democracy have come into some of the churches. This teaching of democracy in the church is a wind of teaching, a devilish blowing of the evil one.

The intention behind the winds of teaching today is twofold: 1) to put down the Lord's present ministry in His recovery; and 2) to oppose the new way, the God-ordained way, which is the scriptural way to meet and to serve for the building up of the Body of Christ. If the God-ordained way and the Lord's present ministry were taken away from us, what would we have left?

Some have said, "We don't need the Life-studies or the notes of the Recovery Version. We can read the pure Word of God." We absolutely need the pure Word of God, but we also need the proper exposition of the Word. How could we have understood the book of Leviticus without the proper exposition? We could read Leviticus again and again without understanding much of it. Peter's vision in Acts 10 was an expounding of Leviticus. Paul also expounded the book of Leviticus in Hebrews. Throughout the centuries of church history, certain brothers have been raised up to expound Leviticus. Today we are "standing on their shoulders" to inherit all of their findings and understanding. By the Lord's mercy, standing upon their shoulders, we have also seen something further. What we have seen is in today's *Life-study of Leviticus*. To say that we do not need such an exposition of the holy Word is a strong wind of teaching blowing the saints away from the central lane of God's economy.

Another wind of teaching today is the teaching that there is no spiritual father. Some have indicated that Paul should not have said in 1 Corinthians 4:15, "For though you have ten thousand guides in Christ, yet not many fathers; for in Christ Jesus I have begotten you through the gospel." To indicate this way, that Paul should not have said that he was the Corinthians' spiritual father, is to overthrow the authority of the Bible.

The Intrinsic Factor of Such Blowing Teachings

With the winds of teaching there is talk about the Bible and about spiritual things, but what is the intrinsic factor of such teaching? In 1933 a brother among us received a note from Brother Watchman Nee that said, "Do the right thing in the right way with the right spirit." This word became a wonderful saying to me. I need to remember all the time to do the right thing in the right way with the right spirit. The things that are being done today related to these winds of teaching are not the right thing, they are not done in the right way, and they are not done in the right spirit. What is being done is wrong, the way is wrong, and the spirit in which it is done is even more wrong. What is being spoken in the winds of teaching are either entire lies or half-truths, which are also lies. Half-truths and innuendos are more evil than a straight lie. The intrinsic factor of such blowing teachings is the sleight of men—man's subtle ways of cheating. The sleight of men is the craftiness of men with a view to a system of error—man's plotted deception to induce people into the satanic system of error (Eph. 4:14). The system of error is of the enemy, Satan.

THE PURPOSE OF THE WINDS OF TEACHING

Now we need to go on to see the purpose of the winds of teaching. The purpose of the winds of teaching is the evil purpose of the enemy Satan, which is versus the eternal economy of God. Their purpose is to overthrow the faith of some believers. Some of the saints' faith has been overthrown by the winds of teaching. They may not oppose the Lord's recovery, but they have lost their faith in the Lord's recovery. They are neutral. They do not come to the meetings regularly, and they are not so concerned about the Lord's interest as they once were. They have been spoiled.

The purpose of the winds of teaching is to devastate the church life (Acts 8:3). This is what Saul of Tarsus did before he became Paul the apostle. Also, the purpose of the winds of teaching is to frustrate the building up of the organic Body of Christ, to tear down the building up of the organic Body of Christ, and to divide the members of the organic Body of Christ—causing endless divisions (sects) in hatred and jealousy, instead of keeping the unique oneness of the Body of Christ in love and kindness (1 Cor. 1:10-11). According to our past history, the instigators of any storm in the recovery all became very divisive. They even divide among themselves. Their division is endless. There is no love or kindness with them. What they do is full of hatred and jealousy.

Now we have seen the purpose of the winds of teaching and their intrinsic factor, which is the sleight of men in craftiness with a view to bring people, to usher people, into a satanic system of error. Those who get brought into Satan's system of error are finished with the building up of the Body of Christ in the central lane of God's New Testament economy.

I am so thankful to the Lord that the majority of the saints in the churches have the proper discernment. They will not be shaken, tossed about, or carried away. Thank the Lord that we are still here in the advance of His recovery today!

ABOUT THE AUTHOR

Witness Lee was born in 1905 in northern China and raised in a Christian family. At age nineteen he was fully captured for Christ and immediately consecrated himself to preach the gospel for the rest of his life. Early in his service, he met Watchman Nee, a renowned preacher, teacher, and writer. Witness Lee labored together with Watchman Nee under his direction. In 1934 Watchman Nee entrusted Witness Lee with the responsibility for his publication operation, called the Shanghai Gospel Book Room.

Prior to the Communist takeover in 1949, Witness Lee was sent by Watchman Nee and his other co-workers to Taiwan to ensure that the things delivered to them by the Lord would not be lost. Watchman Nee instructed Witness Lee to continue the former's publishing operation abroad as the Taiwan Gospel Book Room, which has been publicly recognized as the publisher of Watchman Nee's works outside China. Witness Lee's work in Taiwan manifested the Lord's abundant blessing. From a mere three hundred fifty believers, newly fled from the mainland, the churches in Taiwan grew to twenty thousand believers in five years.

In 1962 Witness Lee felt led of the Lord to move to the United States, and he began to minister in Los Angeles in December of that year. During his thirty-five years of service throughout the United States, he ministered in weekly meetings, weekend conferences, and weeklong trainings, delivering several thousand spoken messages. His speaking has since been published, and many of his books have been translated into numerous languages. He gave his last public conference in February 1997 at the age of ninety-one and went to be with the Lord, whom he loved and served, on June 9, 1997. Witness Lee leaves behind a prolific presentation of the truth in the Bible. His major work, *Life-study of the Bible,* the fruit of his labor from 1974 to 1995, comprises over twenty-five thousand pages of commentary on every book of the Bible from the perspective of the believers' enjoyment and experience of God's divine life in Christ through the Holy Spirit. In addition, *The Collected Works of Witness Lee* contains over one hundred thirty volumes (over seventy-five thousand pages) of his other ministry from 1932 to 1997. Witness Lee was also the chief editor of a new translation of the New Testament into Chinese called the Recovery Version, and he directed the translation of the English New Testament Recovery Version. The Recovery Version also appears in over twenty-five other languages. In the Recovery Version he provided an extensive body of footnotes, outlines, and spiritual cross references. A radio broadcast of his messages can be heard on Christian radio stations in the United States and Europe. In 1965 Witness Lee founded Living Stream Ministry, a non-profit corporation, located in Anaheim, California, which publishes his and Watchman Nee's ministry.

Witness Lee's ministry emphasizes the experience of Christ as life and the practical oneness of the believers as the Body of Christ. Stressing the importance of attending to both of these matters, he led the churches under his care to grow in Christian life and function. He was unbending in his conviction that God's goal is not narrow sectarianism but the universal Body of Christ. In time, believers everywhere began to meet simply as the church in their localities in response to this conviction. Through his ministry hundreds of local churches have been raised up throughout the earth.

OTHER BOOKS PUBLISHED BY
Living Stream Ministry

Titles by Witness Lee:

Titles by Watchman Nee:

Available at
Christian bookstores, or contact Living Stream Ministry
2431 W. La Palma Ave. • Anaheim, CA 92801
1-800-549-5164 • www.livingstream.com